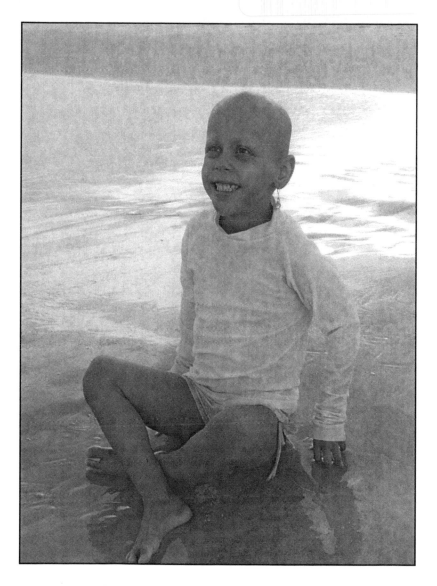

A True Story About A Miracle in Miami

Why Me?

Raymond Rodriguez-Torres, M.mgt

WESTBOW
PRESS

Author photo courtesy of Adrifoto.com

WestBow Press books may be ordered through booksellers or by contacting:

WestBow Press
A Division of Thomas Nelson
1663 Liberty Drive
Bloomington, IN 47403
www.westbowpress.com
1-(866) 928-1240

ISBN: 978-1-4497-0301-1 (sc)
ISBN: 978-1-4497-0302-8 (hc)
ISBN: 978-1-4497-0300-4 (e)

Library of Congress Control Number: 2010929971

Printed in the United States of America

WestBow Press rev. date: 6/29/2010

Acknowledgements

To God, the Almighty Father, to Jesus, our Lord, savior, and healer and to the Holy Spirit who have made this miracle and this book possible. To Our Lady of Guadalupe, "Mommy Church", we love you and thank you for your intercession and always being with Bella.

To all who are battling cancer, especially our children: You are angels that come to earth to show us how to live. Your courage is immeasurable; your faith is inspiring. You are real world super heroes for the entire world to admire. Indeed, the definition of courage can be seen at a pediatric cancer center.

To my loving, courageous, beautiful, and dedicated wife Shannah, thank you for always believing in me, for always challenging me, and always telling me the truth. I love you and am forever grateful God brought us, and kept us together against all odds.

To my most precious girls: Bella and Rayna. I love you beyond words.

To my parents: Ramon and Guly. Thank you for your unconditional love, life long support, exemplary parenting and belief in me that I can accomplish anything God directs me to do. I am forever your loving and grateful son.

To Ralph and Kim: (Our "Drino and Drina") there are little words to express our appreciation for the blessing that you are. Your love for us is a direct reflection of the love and sacrifice of Christ. Thank you for the constant example of faith, for giving of yourself unselfishly and completely to us during our most difficult trial. You have, and continue to embody the love of God not only to us, but to everyone you come in contact with. Thank you, we love you and are eternally grateful.

To my extended family: thank you for your love, support, and continued fervent prayers. To the Missionary Sisters of the

Immaculate Heart of Mary: Catalina, Silvia, and Dolores: Thank you for your constant prayers and love.

To Monsignor Navarro, our parish priests, and our entire St. John Neumann Parish family: there are too many to name. Bless you and thank you for welcoming us with open hearts and open arms. We are forever grateful for your prayers, generosity, and love of Bella and our family.

To the many angels that God put in our path: You know who you are. Thank you for opening your hearts, your homes, and your lives to us and to the miracle of Bella. May the Lord bless you and yours abundantly for all you have and continue to do for Bella and our family.

To the army of people in prayer all over the world: ("Bella's Believers") Thank you! Thank you for being part of this miracle. Thank you for standing on this battlefield with us and standing in agreement that NOTHING is impossible for God. Thank you for believing in the power of prayer, for your incredible generosity, and unconditional support.

To Drs., Escalon, Pefkarou, Kahtib, Fort, De Angulo, McDowell, Sandler, Altman, Melnick, Papazian, Granado-Villar, and Keole we love you, thank you for your dedication, love, and support! To Dr. Meister, Dr. Botero, Dr. Wexler and Dr. Kramer, although you had not yet taken care of Bella during the time frame of this book, thank you and bless you for all you have and continue to do for Bella and our family. To all of the amazing, selfless, nurses, and caretakers of Bella: We are forever grateful for your dedication and kindness.

To Katy Hibbard, Elsie Valderrama: and the many who edited and contributed to this book. Thank you! May this work bless everyone who reads it.

To the reader: Thank you for purchasing this book. 100% of my profits from this book are being donated to pediatric cancer research and to charity.

With my deepest appreciation and love,
Raymond Rodriguez-Torres, M.mgt

VICTORY IN CHRIST!

Foreword by Monsignor Pablo A. Navarro

Happiness and joy are very relative for many people. Some equate happiness and joy with material possessions, others with health and peace; still others have varied barometers for "happiness." People often pray for the "miracle" that will bring them ultimate happiness and joy. Of course, such a "miracle" does not exist. The only wonderful miracle that God constantly gives is the happiness of knowing that we are not 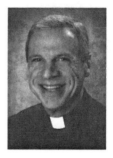 alone....God is always with us. Even when we feel the most alone.... that is when God is most present in a subtle and gentle way.

Miracles happen constantly all around us. We just need to open our eyes to see what God is doing. God's goodness is all around us, much like radio waves. However, unless our heart's "receiver" is tuned and synchronized to the "God-waves" we can easily miss them.

In this work; *"Why Not Me?"* Raymond Rodriguez-Torres pokes at and confronts us with the reality of the works of God in his life and the life of his family through the words and "miracle" of a child.

For those who find it hard to believe; for those who wish to believe; the witness of *"Why Not Me"* will be both moving and stimulating.....a must read.....it was for me.

Monsignor Pablo A. Navarro

Contents

I'M SURE IT'S NOTHING SERIOUS.

The morning of July 11, 2007, began like many others. I woke up in a different city in another hotel room. On this day it happened to be Orlando, Florida, which was nice because I was closer to home. Soon I would be back home spending some quality time with my girls, Bella, Rayna, and Shannah.

I was preparing for a meeting and looking forward to catching my short flight back home to Miami at 3:00 PM after my half-day meeting. At the time I worked as an executive for a multinational company, and I traveled quite often.

At 7:00 am, I called home and spoke to my very tired and worried wife, Shannah. She told me they had experienced a terrible night. Bella, my oldest, who was four and a half years old at the time, had complained all night of stomach pain, was getting up frequently to go out to the living room, and kept tripping and falling to the floor. By now Bella could not stand, and Shannah was very concerned. I could sense fear and panic in her voice. Now, my wife always feels a greater sense of security when I am home, but I could tell by the tone of her voice that she was deeply concerned. It was more than just the "wish you were home" type of tone. I tried my best to ease her worry, and told her it might just be a virus that had temporarily entered the spinal fluid, and that she should take Bella to the hospital. But not to worry, I told her. I was sure it wasn't anything too serious.

Shannah had already spoken to my father, a pediatrician and the former chief of staff of Miami Children's Hospital, who was on his way to my house to examine Bella. Bella had been complaining of a bellyache for the last several days, but she had been seen by her pediatrician, a Gastroenterologist and an Emergency Physician. She had had an abdominal X-ray and an ultrasound. It was found that she had gas, and we were instructed to give her laxatives to alleviate the bothersome lingering discomfort. There did not seem to be anything of any major concern.

At 9:00 AM, I spoke with my father, who had already managed to get to the hospital with Bella and Shannah. He was concerned. He explained that they were planning to perform a lumbar puncture on Bella to examine the condition of the spinal fluid. I know it may be standard protocol to do a lumbar puncture, but the sheer thought of having a large needle inserted into my little girl's spine was not exactly what I thought this day would bring me. I felt very helpless not being able to be there and take charge, the way I normally would. The thought of Shannah and Bella at the hospital without me made me very uneasy.

I decided I should leave my meeting and go home. I informed my boss at the time, Sheri Jepsen, who is an absolute angel, what was happening and that I thought it would be best if I left. She agreed and actually adjourned the entire meeting. I am very grateful for her compassion, because I know few supervisors would be as understanding and accommodating.

I called American Airlines to see which earlier flights were available. There was a 1:00 PM flight I could get on; I asked the operator to please change my ticket. She informed me there was no record of my ticket for the 3:00 PM flight. I informed the operator that I had my actual printed boarding pass for the 3:00 PM flight with me; how could the system show that I had no ticket for the flight? After much back-and-forth, she informed me I would have to go to the airport to resolve my issue. I kept thinking there must just be some type of computer glitch and that it would easily be resolved as soon as I arrived at the airport. Two of my colleagues,

Shari Mitchell and Cliff Jones, who were also going to the airport, dropped me off.

As we arrived at the terminal, my cell phone rang; it was my father. He told me the neurologist believed Bella had Guillain Barre Syndrome. This news hit me like a shockwave. I was caught off guard. Surely there had to be some mistake. This couldn't possibly be true. My little girl was doing okay when I left home. She simply had an upset stomach or a simple virus. The doctor must have made a mistake. I immediately turned white and almost began to cry in the car right in front of my colleagues. They noticed my reaction to the call. I looked at them and my voice trembled as I said, "She has a terrible disease," and I exited the car.

I entered the Orlando airport in shock. I focused on getting home and getting on the earlier flight back to Miami. I figured once I get home things would get better. I would resolve this mistake when I got to the hospital. It simply couldn't be true. Bella is fine!

I am all too familiar with Guillain Barre Syndrome. My father suffered from it in 1995. I will never forget when my father was diagnosed. At that time, an exact treatment for Guillain Barre Syndrome (GBS) was not known. What *was* known is that it was a terrible illness in which the immune system attacks the neurological system. Consequently, paralysis begins in the lower extremities and moves up toward the lungs. The major cause of death in these cases is that the respiratory system can become paralyzed, and patients die or have to be put on a ventilator. How could this possibly be what Bella has?

When my father was diagnosed, I was studying in Gainesville at the University of Florida. I was living the carefree days of college—a little time studying and a lot more partying. Life was good, and I was busy collecting memories of a lifetime. Why was my peace being disturbed? When I learned of his hospitalization, I immediately drove to Miami. I was afraid my father was going to die, and I was only nineteen years old. I remember praying, *Lord, please don't take him now. I'm not old or mature enough; I need him here.* I was scared to death of what could happen to my father. The news came very suddenly and without any warning.

When I arrived at the hospital where my father was, I anxiously took the elevator and headed toward my father's room. I can never forget my experience trying to enter that room. I could see my dad in the room, lying in the bed, and as I tried to enter, he, from a distance, asked me not to enter at that moment. My father's attorney, who I was surprised to see, immediately closed the door in my face. My father was in the process of updating his last will and testament. I was confused; my heart rate began to rise and my palms began to sweat. How could this be happening? God, why? I sat outside the room, alone and very scared, waiting for someone to allow me in.

My father, as a physician, had diagnosed himself and knew very well the consequences of GBS. Once I was able to enter the room, my father told me that GBS was a serious illness, which he knew by faith that the Lord would heal him from. However, it behooved him to ensure that everything was in order for our family. It was a very uncertain and scary time in 1995.

It was surreal that Bella was now dealing with the same illness and I was in Orlando and not with her. By the grace of God, my father recovered fully after only two months and has never suffered any recurrence.

I approached the airline counter at the Orlando airport scared and with a tear in my eye. I tried to keep my composure, but my emotions got the better of me. The telephone operator of the airline, prior to my arrival, had informed me that the flight I was trying to get on was full. I pleaded with the attendant behind the desk. I explained that my daughter was very ill and was going to be transferred to critical care in Miami. I told her I needed a straight answer on whether I was going to make the flight on standby. I told her that if I was not to make the flight to please tell me right there so I could rent a car and drive the four hours rather than wait for the later flight I was supposed to be on. My emotions overwhelmed me. I felt like grabbing the woman and shaking her violently so that she could understand my state of despair. I was only 250 miles from Miami, but I felt like I was as far away as New Zealand. Time just seemed to drag on. Each second seemed an eternity as I tried to resolve the matter and did not appear to be making any headway.

4

At this point I was sobbing, and I could barely speak. The nice lady behind the desk told me to please have a seat and that she would let me know as soon as she could. I found a seat next to the airline counter and began to cry like I never had before. I am a very proud and supposedly strong person. For me to cry like this, especially in public, was something I had never experienced. The tears rolled down my face uncontrollably; there was nowhere I could go, no bathroom, no other waiting area, and no discreet corner. I was sitting there with many people walking in front of me, looking at me in shock. I called my brother Ralph, who is my older brother and is more like a second father to me, and he did not answer. I later learned he was serving on jury duty and was confined to the courtroom at the time I was desperately trying to reach him. I called my friend Andy—my oldest friend—who is an attorney. He was in court and could not speak but told me, "Take it easy, I'll call you in a little while; everything will be okay." I called my friend Jose, whom I have known since third grade, and could hardly speak. He told me he was in a lunch meeting and would call me back.

I felt as though there was no one to calm me. I was alone. I had never felt so alone. Imagine yourself hitting a roadblock with every step you take. This was how it felt. It was agony, and it felt like an eternity before I finally got my response.

A few moments later, the attendant at the desk called my name. She handed me a first-class boarding pass and told me, "I hope all goes well with your daughter." I almost fell to my knees when she gave me this wonderful news! Thank God, things were finally starting to improve. I made the flight and was on my way to Miami, headed straight for Miami Children's Hospital.

A FOUNDATION OF FAITH

When I was 9 years old, I read the words that would stay with me forever: "God's Gift to you is who you are; your gift to Him is who you become." I found this in the most inconspicuous place, in a corner of my oldest friend's kitchen. Even though this small plaque was in a hard to see corner, I have spent all of my life trying to understand what my gift to Him was to be. I have always known that I wanted to become a good man, defined by those standards and attributes of the people I have admired or who where considered good by society and the world. I have always felt that I had to continuously improve my social standing, my financial and professional standing and lastly, increase my faith and good deeds in order to become who I thought I was to be. Because of those words I read when I was nine, I have continuously strived to become better, albeit with many mistakes along the way, I have always kicked myself to do more. But what exactly? Thus far in my life, thank God, I have succeeded in business, financially, and in my social standing but have still felt a feeling that I have something greater to do. On the surface the message seems so simple, yet I feel there is a deep and profound message that goes much beyond what I can easily identify.

At the time I write this, I am 33 years old. Many who know me say that I have experienced life way beyond my years. I indeed have been blessed to have experienced many episodes in life both pleasant and unpleasant which make me who I am today. While the many experiences I have faced in life make for interesting story telling, I have always reflected in my most private moments, who am I becoming?

A wise man once said "in order to understand the present, you must understand the past. If you want to delve into looking at the future, you must first have a clear understanding of the present." That wise man is my father. In order for me to describe who I am and what has enabled and compelled me to write this book, I must tell you who I am and how I came to be.

I am the son of Ramon Rodriguez-Torres and Guly Rodriguez-Torres, immigrants to the United States from Cuba. My father is a pediatrician and a pediatric cardiologist, a great man by many standards, a man of great faith and my best friend. My father attended medical school in Cuba and began his practice of adult medicine and cardiology in Havana. He later founded a large clinic (private hospital) in Havana which was thriving until the ascent to power of Fidel Castro. At the time of the clinic's founding, my father had just returned to Cuba from specialized training in Cardiology at the University of Manchester and the Royal Infirmary at London, England. One morning two years prior, he read in the newspaper about a scholarship that the British Council was offering for qualified Cuban professionals to study a variety of subjects at the University of Manchester. There was to be an exam and that the candidate with the highest score would be offered, if he met several other requirements, the scholarship. My father knew that this scholarship was to be his the very moment he read the advertisement. He had one major problem however, it was not his medical knowledge or his fear of leaving my mother and brothers to go to England, it was that he did not speak English!

Nonetheless, he was determined and began to study English both on his own and with 2 British tutors. He eventually learned enough English to be able to take the exam. The Lord looked upon him with favor and my father scored the highest of 64 applicants and won the scholarship. He was overjoyed and went off to Manchester, England for one year to study cardiology and experience some of the coldest nights of his life living in a boarding house for exchange students in Manchester. While in England, my father had the privilege of studying under Dr. Paul Wood, who at the time was one of the most renowned clinical cardiologists in the world. This separation from his homeland in the Caribbean to a far and distant land was not easy for my father. As most Cubans, he was raised in a very close knit family and he greatly missed my mother, my grandparents, and my eldest brother. My mother visited my father once while in England, and was able to cook my father his favorite Cuban dish, "picadillo." This was a great lifting for my father since he never could adjust to British cuisine, of particular dislike, cabbage.

It was a challenging time for my mother being alone in Cuba working and taking care of my oldest bother who was a young child at the time. She missed my father and she knew he greatly missed her too. It was a heartfelt challenge to be without him, Nonetheless she knew it was for the best and she had faith that God would continue to bless them and guide them and my father. Eventually my father was able to complete his cardiology program in Manchester and return to his native Cuba.

In February of 1960, my father was invited to attend a dinner party at the home of a fellow cardiologist of Havana. He was excited to attend the party as the fellow doctor was a friend and her husband was the secretary of state. It was a party where there where only a few people in attendance. Much to everyone's surprise at approximately 11:00 PM, Fidel Castro arrived. At the time, he had recently taken power in Cuba and was a well known revolutionary promising equality between the classes and reform compared to the government under Batista. At this party, Castro gave a speech in which he expressed his intentions for the future of Cuba. My father immediately recognized Castro's plan as socialism disguised by his true intentions of becoming the eventual dictator of Cuba. The following morning, my father said he made what he thought was the biggest mistake of this life: he called for a meeting of his shareholders (the other doctors who comprised the clinic) and explained to them what had occurred the night before, how he met Castro and what his true intentions where. My father implored them to join him and do whatever they could as physicians and upstanding members of society in Havana to prevent Castro's plans. He immediately learned that all of his partners were in favor of Castro. In fact, many had already been promised high level government positions including ministry head positions by Castro and his followers. In addition much to my father's surprise, his shareholders told him how when he was away in England, the clinic supported many functions in favor of Castro. Furthermore, one of my father's closest friends and the partner which helped him found the clinic from a small operation to an expanding 13 story building asked my father to reconsider. He said to him "Ramon, all those concerns you have will go away once you read this." He pulled out a little red booklet from his briefcase; it was a book about the communist theory of Mao Tse Tung. My father immediately realized that his partners where for Castro and that he had just expressed to them how adamantly against Castro and all those that followed him he was. As you can imagine, as the president of a growing medical clinic in Havana both in medical prestige and financially, my father was the target of jealousy. Now that my father had and continued to express his disapproval of Castro, those who wished to have control of the clinic began to rally against my father and move in favor of Fidel Castro.

Over the course of the months that followed, my parent's life became increasingly difficult. Their situation at home changed significantly also as my middle brother Ralph was born in March of 1960. As Castro put his plan into action, life in Cuba became more unstable and my parents began to realize that all they had worked for and the future they thought they had was uncertain. My parents are very peaceful people; in fact, my father is the greatest example of Christ on earth I have ever met. He is a man of great compassion and of extremely high moral values. He beholds a great deal of integrity, dignity and is one the most ethical individuals you could ever meet. Yet, those who knew my father was against Castro's revolution and had ulterior motives of removing him as president of the clinic began to make up stories about my parents and accuse them of aiding Batista and being against the revolution. My parent's home was frequently searched for weapons in the middle of the

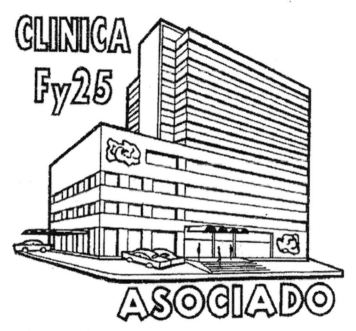

An Architect's rendering of my father's clinic. CIRCA1960, Havana, Cuba

night. They were interrogated frequently and questioned as to their allegiance to the revolution. In short, life was taking a very difficult turn for them and all they knew was rapidly falling apart. Life as they knew it had taken a drastic change and it did not appear that it would change anytime soon.

It took eight months for my father to come to the realization that they would have to leave their beloved Cuba. They would have to leave everything they had built; they would have to leave everyone they knew. They understood that they could not live under a dictatorship, they wanted and stood for freedom and they knew then that they would not be free under Castro. It was by far, one of the most difficult decisions that would ever be faced with but freedom was simply too big a price to pay.

As my parents prepared their secret plans to leave Cuba, they knew that they could tell no one. No one could be trusted and they would have to exit in a way that was as inconspicuous as possible. It was hard to come to the realization that they would have to leave everything behind, leave the country and re-establish themselves wherever they landed. While the decision to leave had been made, it still caused a great deal of anxiety and despair and a great many sleepless nights thinking about an uncertain but hopeful future.

My father decided that the island of Puerto Rico would be where they could flee. It was part of the United States and a place where the language spoken is Spanish. In addition, my father knew that wherever he went he would have to start as an intern. He learned that, at that time in the continental U.S., medical interns, despite their prior qualifications, were being paid $50 per month. In Puerto Rico, the pay for an intern was $150 per month.

Because they had to be inconspicuous, my father bought an airline ticket under the premise that he would be attending a medical conference in Puerto Rico. He would be traveling alone. My mother, my two older brothers, and my paternal grandparents would not leave Cuba until the following afternoon on supposed vacation and would meet him in Puerto Rico. This way they would not all be leaving at once and would not seem as they were defecting the island. When my parents left Cuba, no one knew, not anyone at the clinic, not the staff my parents had working and living in their home, not even members of their own family.

Because you were only allowed to leave with the equivalent of $5, my mother and my grandmother sewed secret pockets in their underwear so they could smuggle bills in large denominations to have some money albeit minimal in Puerto Rico. My mother removed the cotton filling from the buttons on her blouse and filled it with dollar bills; she also stuffed plastic fruits on her hat with bills. Some members of our family went as far as smuggling some jewelry by swallowing it. People who were fleeing the island nation were forced to become creative in their efforts to take more money with them. How can anyone even attempt to establish a new life in a new country with a mere $5? Of course, this was just one strong deterrent that the government used to get those wanting to leave to think twice.

On the evening of October 10, 1960, my father left Cuba and landed in San Juan, Puerto Rico. He had nothing but what he carried with him. He tried to leave Cuba with the equivalent of $150 US dollars, yet when he was interviewed and searched at the airport in Havana, the money was confiscated and he was only given $5 dollars. He explained that he was attending a medical conference and that he needed the money he brought with him, for the registration fee for the conference, but it was to no avail. While he was on the flight to Puerto Rico, he was worried as to where he would stay. His money had been confiscated and he could not afford a hotel with only $5 dollars. His plan was to go the secretary of health of Puerto Rico the following day and plead his case as a physician and seek employment. He had no hotel and nowhere to stay. He intended to sleep in a public park in the Condado area; he was familiar with this area as being safe from other visits to Puerto Rico while on vacation in the past. Here was a man who had worked and prepared himself for a very successful life. He had accomplished a great many things and made great leaps from his humble beginnings as a boy in Cuba and was planning to possibly spend the night sleeping on a bench in a public park in Puerto Rico. Needless to say he landed at Luis

Munoz Marin airport, fearful of what might happen to him. He was alone, or so he thought. God was with him.

During the previous year, one of my father's friends back in Cuba had a daughter who had recently married an Englishman who was quite wealthy and was doing a significant amount of business in the Caribbean during those years. While my father did met the gentleman during several family social gatherings, they were certainly not close by any means.

As my father walked through the airport terminal in San Juan on that October evening in 1960, he noticed someone smiling at him from a distance. It was a man who waived him over; it was the Englishman who had recently married my father's friend's daughter. Surprised to see my father there he said "Ramon, what are you doing here?" My father responded "I have defected Cuba, I have left everything." The gentleman was in disbelief, his first question was to ask my father what hotel he would be staying at. My father answered "I have no hotel; I am planning to sleep in a park tonight." If you knew my father, you would know how difficult it must have been for him to say this to this man. My father is a gracious, wise, hardworking and proud man, a visionary who always has a plan. For him to admit that he was going to sleep in a park was very difficult.

While I don't know many details about this gentleman, I do know that this was the work of God. What are the chances that almost out of the blue this man would appear? It was no coincidence that this man was at that airport on that evening. That night and the following morning, this man helped my father; he lent my father the money necessary to rent a house, furnish it and have food in the refrigerator before my mother, brothers and grandparents arrived.

By the grace of God, my father was granted an appointment with the secretary of health the very next day, October 11th 1960. As my father pleaded his case to the secretary of health, he informed my father that the only thing he had available was an intern position in an Emergency Room in Fajardo under the supervision of Dr. Jose Soler-Zapata. My father immediately went to Fajardo to meet Dr. Soler-Zapata. Dr. Soler-Zapata graciously informed my father that if he wanted the job he could have it, although as a fully licensed cardiologist he was technically over qualified. The job was his and he was on call that very night. My father and entire family will forever be indebted to Dr. Soler-Zapata, the person that the Lord put in my father's path opening his first opportunity after leaving Cuba. Dr. Soler-Zapata eventually became the Secretary of Health of Puerto Rico and his love, affection, and support for my family and me long continued after my parent's departure from Puerto Rico and eventual migration to the continental United States.

While my father was pleased to have employment in Puerto Rico, he did desire to practice medicine in the United States. He eagerly sent letters and his curriculum vitae to several hospitals and institutions in the U.S. His efforts eventually paid off.

At the completion of one year in Puerto Rico, my father was offered and accepted a position at Downstate Medical Center-State University of New York in Brooklyn, New York. There he started all over again, having to prove himself clinically in a challenging and competitive academic environment. As if that was not enough, during that time (early and mid 60s) my parents found themselves in a country which was undergoing much change and uncertainty. The United States was at war with Vietnam, there was much social-political unrest with the war and other social issues, which were foreign to my parents. They lived in a small apartment in Brooklyn and at first had very little means. Living in a small apartment with a wife, two small children, and his parents was not exactly the life that my father had envisioned. However, he had always been such a determined individual that he knew it was just a temporary situation. The U.S. was the land of opportunity and those who came with the proper mindset and a spirit of overcoming obstacles were certain to be successful. My father initially worked as an assistant for the Chief of Pediatric Cardiology who was also a man facing turmoil. The environment at the University was competitive and he was in an enviable position. This man found himself under extreme pressure and often took out his frustrations on his staff. Four days after my father began working at the University this man took out his frustration on my father and yelled at him to get an extension cord for a presentation in front of the medical staff and several hundred medical and surgical students.

As I mentioned before, my father is a great man, he is wise, patient and even tempered. However, because my father would never intentionally embarrass or purposely hurt someone else, on the few occasions in his life where it has been done to him, he has been filled with overwhelming frustration. This episode of the electrical cord was one of those times.

My father quietly retrieved the extension cord and the presentation went on as planned. After he finished his work in the evening he returned home. He could not sleep, he was lying in bed wondering why he was in this situation, why God had forsaken him, why was he laying in a cheap apartment building, answering to a bully and borderline incompetent man, why did he have to leave all the comforts of his life in Cuba to come and now be in a country which was in it's own turmoil. He also recognized that there was no turning back, no room for failure, no giving up. He had to make it! No matter how bad his Spanish accent was, no matter how bad the situation in the US was regarding Vietnam, this was his new life. He had faith that God had put him there for a reason, he had faith that he would provide the kind of life he had in Cuba if not better for his family and he knew that the Lord had called him to be a physician to help save lives. As he lay in bed, he was thinking of how he was going to deal with his boss. He could not and would not allow another man to treat him with disrespect. He understood that, he had to do what he had to do and would serve this man, the university, the patients and the students to the best of his abilities', but he could not stand to be yelled at or be humiliated.

The next morning, my father arrived at the university at 6:00 AM. He sat inside his boss's office waiting for him. When the man arrived he was shocked to see my father sitting in his office. My father asked him to come in and sit down. He looked at him in the eye and said "I lost all I had in Cuba. I lost my home, I lost my friends, and I lost my hospital and everything I knew. The only thing I have never lost is my self respect. Sir, I understand you are the chief, and I am honored to work here and to work for you, but I cannot allow under any circumstance for you or anyone here to ever yell at me or demean me, I simply cannot stand for it. I promise I will serve you with humility and I will do whatever you ask, however we must have a profound understanding, right here and right now that what you did yesterday will not so much as cross your mind ever again. Understand this- I have to make it, there is no turning back for me, this is all I have, I must and will succeed!"

His boss was speechless, but did apologize and fully understood that my father was sincere and committed in his statements. A few months after this incident, this man was unfortunately forced to resign. My father was named Chief of Pediatric Cardiology. You can imagine the politics, jealousy and fallout that occurred when my father, who was a "nobody" with a heavy Spanish accent, was named chairman over a long line of tenured and distinguished professors who spent years vying for the position. In fact, one of the very first challenges that he faced was that he was asked by a professor to teach as a guest speaker one of his first year medical school classes. This class held roughly 200 students. It was a rowdy group which frequently protested the war, the university and anything else, right in the middle of class. It was not uncommon for people to light cigarettes and smoke marijuana during a lecture. It was a debacle. The professor who invited my father to speak probably figured it would be a big joke to have my father with this heavy accent try to address and manage this group. It certainly would have been quite an embarrassment for the newly appointed chief to fall on his face.

When my father entered the room, he noticed many of the students were not wearing shoes and some were sitting on the floor. He was shocked at the scene before him. This was very different from his experience at the University of Havana, let alone the pristine and traditional setting at the University of Manchester in England. As he stood at the podium and began to address the crowd, the few that were paying attention began to laugh loudly and make fun of my father's accent. There was much noise and commotion in the room. He paused for a moment and said in a loud voice; "I will wait for you!"

He remained at the podium very still and composed. The noise eventually died down and the room became quiet; you could hear a pin drop. He eventually spoke after a long period of uncomfortable silence. He said to them "Ladies and Gentlemen, the beauty of my lecture is that it is optional for you. You don't have to be here, in fact I would prefer that some of you were not here, and in a moment I will ask some of you to leave. This lecture is going to cost you more than the tuition you have already paid. In fact, looking around the room, I can tell this is going to be perhaps the most expensive lecture some of you have heard. I say this because should you decide to stay, you will have to pay a price. I feel it is only fair, since I am going to impart on you years of experience in treating patients and saving lives. Indeed your future patients would be paying a price if they would happen to be under your care, so now you must pay a price for this lecture. If you are to stay in this room and listen to what I am going to say, albeit with my thick accent, you will immediately agree to the following:

If you are smoking, you must immediately extinguish all cigarettes. I will not allow this in this room, under any circumstance. You must sit in a chair, you will fix your clothing to be presentable, if you are not wearing shoes, you must leave or find some right now, there is to be no talking or laughing, and lastly and most importantly, you must want to have a genuine desire to learn and to put others, particularly your future patients, before yourself or even your own families. You are about to embark on the profession of being a physician. This is the profession that requires you to care for others before yourself. I can assure you that this responsibility is not for everyone. In fact, if you are not sure that you should be here, if you feel that your time and talents would be better spent elsewhere or if you cannot adhere to the rules or pay the price I have just described, then I will pause for a moment for all of you to reflect on what I have just said. I will also wait for those of you that will be leaving to collect your belongings. Lastly, I will wait for those of you that choose to stay and pay the price of this lecture to prepare yourselves to listen and learn!"

The room was stunned. There was absolute silence. There he stood again steadfast and silent. There was some commotion, but no one left the auditorium. The students got off the floor, put on their shoes, adjusted their clothing and did as he asked. At the end of a very educational and motivating lecture, my father exited the auditorium to a standing ovation. Yet again, he proved his resolve to succeed and teach others to help and heal mankind.

My father had proven himself as chief of Pediatric Cardiology. He was gaining the respect of those who doubted him because of his selfless nature and genuine interest in saving lives. My father inspired those around him with a new sense of purpose, a renewed desire to conduct clinical research and innovate healthcare. My father's department began to work in areas never before been studied. Needless to say, professionally things where going quite well.

In the personal arena my family was adjusting to life in the U.S. While the country certainly offered freedom, and opportunity not found in Cuba or anywhere else in the world, the issues surrounding the war in Vietnam continued to perpetuate an environment of uncertainty. In fact, the situation was so tumultuous living in Brooklyn during that time for my parents that my father began to think to himself: I have left everything; here I am in a country which appears very unstable. If something similar to what happened in Cuba should happen here, the first people that will be in trouble will be immigrants like me. My father pondered this for some time. The environment at the University and the ever growing uncertainty of American society had him paranoid that something would happen causing him to pick up and leave everything yet again.

Unbeknown to anyone in our family for over 30 years, my father crossed the American border and drove into Canada alone on a Saturday morning. With the limited financial resources he was able to muster, he negotiated to buy a very small parcel of land. He did not tell my mother or anyone about this until he was 76 years old and living in Miami, Florida. His thinking at that time was that if God forbid anything should happen in the U.S. resembling what happened in Cuba, or if for any reason he and my family found themselves in a situation where they would have to flee again, they could drive to the Canadian border and prove that they owned land and would be granted entry.

You can imagine the level of healthy paranoia and vision someone has to have to do something like this. I say healthy paranoia because it was this paranoia, and more so, the Holy Spirit's lead that gave my father the vision to leave Cuba. Indeed, his steps were being guided, perhaps what aided him to make such a drastic decision was his knowledge that earlier his clinic back in Havana had been turned into government housing and was no longer a medical facility. Sadly, many of his friends who stayed and were so adamantly in favor of Castro were not living out their promised positions of power with the new administration. Many of them were in prison and others were now trying to flee Cuba with great difficulty. Trying to leave Cuba now was even more difficult. By this time the government had confiscated all private property and made it part of the state, the situation in Cuba got worse and many of my parent's friends and families who thought my parents were crazy for leaving everything in 1960 were now dead or in prison.

My father continued his work and passion for heading clinical research in Brooklyn. Over the span of 15 years he and his team published over 20 articles and made several breakthroughs to advance medical care. One such advancement, which the Lord led my father to accomplish, was in the area of pediatric intensive care. My father was investigating the high mortality of children while in the intensive care unit (ICU). There was a level of hospital acquired infection in these children which may have been being transmitted by the adults in the same unit. He found that when it came to resuscitation, it was equally a challenge. Most of the biomedical equipment in the I.C.U was always set to adult levels, so in the case of emergency, it took an extra step to set things up for pediatric use.

My father had the idea of establishing a Pediatric Intensive Care Unit. It would be its own stand alone unit, separate from adults and dedicated solely to children. This was a novel idea and not the practice in the United States. In order for this to be accomplished, my father had to ask for an increase of his staff, an expenditure of new medical equipment and space to set up the unit in Kings

County Hospital. My father had proven himself in the past and was granted his request by the state of New York, the City of New York and the administration of the university. My father's purpose was to save lives and prove that better outcomes could be achieved by having a separate PICU.

This was the first PICU in the United States. It was demonstrating early on to be a success, while they did not yet have long term conclusive data the trend they were seeing was that the stand alone PICU was significantly reducing mortality and infection.

One day, the well known NBC television reporter, Frank Field came to do a story about my father and this revolutionary unit just for children. Incredibly, in the middle of the interview, a child went into cardiac arrest. NBC caught live on tape how the members of the PICU and my father stabilized and saved this boy's life. My father's original plan for the PICU is what was used to create these units across the country and what has become the standard of care. Today, most hospitals have their own PICU and thousands upon thousands of children's lives have been saved. A few years later, because of his hard work and dedication, my father was appointed full professor of the State University of New York and Chairman of the Department of Pediatrics.

As my father has aged (he is currently 82 years old) he has shared more with me about what life was like in Brooklyn during those years and what a tumultuous situation this country was in. To hear him describe what they went through in terms of discrimination during the Cuban missile crisis simply because they were Cuban was sadly amazing. Many people who they thought were their friends turned their back on them.

After 15 years at the State University of New York my father was offered and accepted the position of chairman of pediatrics at the Medical College of Ohio in Toledo, Ohio. Life was very different in Toledo when compared to Brooklyn. This was the conservative Midwest and with their heavy Spanish accents, they stuck out even more so. Nonetheless, my family was used to adjusting to change by now. My brothers were now teenagers in high school and were adjusting to their new surroundings and quality of life. My father was working intensely to strengthen the pediatric program in Toledo and things were going relatively well and as planned. While my parent's had their plan, the Lord had a surprise for them. At the age of 43, my mother became pregnant. You can imagine everyone's surprise and joy! My parents were hoping for a girl. In fact, the first child my mother gave birth to back in Cuba was not my oldest brother, it was a little girl. Her name was Carmen and she died of a complication that would be easily resolved today when she was 2 days old. She is buried in Cuba. Since then they only had two boys, my brothers Raul and Ralph and they thought perhaps, now we will have a little girl, how wonderful it would be to finally raise a little girl.

My mother's pregnancy went well and many of the physician's wives at the hospital befriended and helped my mother greatly. They were feeling more comfortable in Toledo and were excited about being older parents with a newborn on the way. Many of the physician families in Toledo were of my parent's age and I suppose that many of them were living vicariously through my parents. The people in Toledo were very kind and loving to my family. As you would expect however, there was another surprise in store.

My mother has never been able to carry a full term pregnancy. My oldest brother, Raul, was born at 7 months and weighed 4 lbs. Ralph was born at 8 months and had no remarkable complications, despite arriving one month early. I was born at 7 months with a severely underdeveloped respiratory system. I weighed 4 pounds at birth and developed a very severe gastrointestinal infection while in the womb. My chances of survival were grim. I was developing new complications on a daily basis and spent my first 26 days of life in the neonatal ICU of Toledo hospital. My parents were devastated, I was very ill and no one thought I was going to live. My parent's horrid memories of having to bury an infant were replaying all over again. I was baptized by a priest in an incubator for fear that I might die. It was hard for my mother to be discharged from the hospital and not take me with her. Each day, they would attend Mass and ask our Lord to spare me from dying.

God's will was for me to recover and fulfill my purpose in life. I recovered and thank the Lord, have been very healthy ever since.

While I weighed only 4 lbs at birth, I grew to be the tallest and heaviest of my brothers.

My parents eventually moved to Miami, Florida where my father served as the Chief of Staff of Miami Children's Hospital for 16 years. While he is now retired from medicine, he continues to work to help his fellow man in all that he does. Growing up in Miami was exciting and unexpected to say the least. In 1980, my mother's family which consists of 8 brothers and sisters and their families came on the Mariel boat lift. This event, sponsored by Castro, allowed a one time offer for anyone wishing to leave Cuba. Castro, of course, used this opportunity to empty his prisons and sent to Miami some of the worst criminals in Cuba. This was best portrayed by the famed movie Scarface. Along with those unsavory characters, came many honest, hardworking Cubans looking for freedom and wishing earnestly to make a new honest living in the United States.

In 1980, my father was faced with a challenging situation. My mother's large family was coming to Miami with nothing and it was up to my parents to help them. My father had the foresight and thankfully the financial means to purchase a small apartment building with 12 units. Growing up as a child I have fond memories of visiting that apartment building with every unit being occupied by aunts, uncles and cousins. Eventually, my father assisted everyone finding jobs, and establishing themselves. They all still live in Miami now and we are a very loving and close knit family.

Indeed I have had a wonderful example of leadership, courage and faith in my parents, my family and particularly in my father. Despite the many challenges and uncertainty they faced, they embraced their situation and succeeded. Rather than thinking "Why me" they thought "Why NOT me" and forged ahead. My father did not hope that he would succeed; he had faith and knew that God had a greater plan for him. This example of faith was the foundation God blessed me with to now fight the greatest battle of my life with what was happening with Bella.

A SON, A HUSBAND, A BROTHER AND FRIEND

Being the baby and surprise child of my family, I have enjoyed many blessings and have equally faced hardship. My childhood could not have been happier. Since my parents were already established in the US, with my father being a physician, my growing up in Miami was much different than that of my brothers, traveling from Cuba when they were very young and later growing up in Puerto Rico, Brooklyn and Ohio.

When my brothers were growing up, my parent's financial situation was challenging. Although they were very young at the time, leaving Cuba and moving frequently was traumatic and tough on my brothers. My brother, Ralph often describes being 4 or 5 years old and not being able to play with the other neighborhood children in Brooklyn, because he didn't speak English. He used to go home and tell my parents that he had learned to speak English. When they asked him to say something in English, Ralph would speak gibberish thinking that he could fool my parents. Children have quite an imagination. My parents stood out with their heavy accents. Also my parents could not afford everything my brothers may have asked them for. While this was difficult for my brothers as children, it was exceptionally difficult on my parents. My mother who once purchased custom clothing for my brother's at the finest boutiques in Havana, was now shopping at the Goodwill and accepting used clothing to dress her boys. Some Saturdays they would drive around looking for clothing and furniture at garage sales or would even take unwanted furniture people would leave on the side of the road. They lived a very simple and humble life, but always strived for more. They always worked harder; they taught their children the value of money and the value of having faith in God.

I too was taught all that my brothers were. To never forget where we came from, never underestimate the value of hard and honest work, but above all, to be thankful to God and to help others as I would one day like to be helped in a time of need. The major difference is that my parents were financially stable and, because of my father's hard work, were in the upper middle class. Growing up, there was nothing I could not have, within reason of course. While I was not always given what I asked for because I was not deserving of it, it was not because my parents could not afford it. When I was sick as an infant my mother made a promise to God that if I survived I was to attend Catholic School until I graduated from high school. She kept her promise and I attended good Catholic schools, had good friends and most importantly began my personal relationship with Jesus Christ.

Our favorite pastime as a family was to go boating. We have been many places on our own boat, both in and outside US waters. We have fished in many fishing tournaments and have seen and visited many wonderful places. While my childhood was privileged by many standards, I was always taught to be thankful, trustworthy, giving and righteous. I was never punished as a child. My parent's instilled in me such a sense of right and wrong that when I misbehaved or had done something wrong, I would be so disappointed that just once glance of disapproval from my father was punishment alone. In short, my childhood was truly blessed.

One of the downsides to being the baby of the family was my parents' age. Growing up, my parents were old compared to other children's parents. I seldom enjoyed playing with my father. He was always at the hospital or away at medical conferences. As a boy I played soccer and was a good player. I played on traveling teams that traveled to Central America and was invited to play in Europe. My mother attended every game, however my father could not attend one. I was never resentful of my father, I understood that he had a greater responsibility and he was and is truly the best father I could have ever been blessed with. Nonetheless, because of my parents' age, I always had a fear that my parents would die when I was young. In fact, when I was born, my brother's were in their late teens. My parent's told them that they had to love me and be ready to care for me if God forbid something happened to them. Further, they implored my brother's to find and marry women that loved and got along with me for the same reason.

I always asked God to please allow me to have my parent's alive until I was at least 20. I felt that at 20 years of age, I could tend to myself, if God forbid something would happen. Needless to say, my parent's are still living and I thank the Lord for them everyday. My father is 83 and my mother is 75 years old. They have been exemplary; have demonstrated to their children, faith, courage, determination and leadership. Another issue I have battled with regarding my parents' age is that I always felt cheated compared to my brothers because I was, in terms of years, the one son who would get to spend the least amount of time with them while they were alive. I wanted my parents to see and know my children. I also did not want to force the issue and have children too early in life simply to fulfill my own purpose and perhaps forsake my children. I have come to learn that quality of time surpasses quantity of time and thank God my parents and my two daughters have a wonderful relationship.

I met the woman I was to marry when I was 19. She was a friend of a friend and at that time I thought she was all wrong for me. I thought I had an idea of the woman that was to be my wife. She was to be Cuban, Catholic, submissive, from a "good" family and a good cook. Little did I know that God has a sense of humor. When I met the woman that eventually would become my wife, she was not a Christian, in fact she was Jewish. She came from a divorced family with several half siblings, was not Cuban, was sassy, hot tempered, did not speak Spanish and could not cook toast without burning it. In short, this was the absolute opposite of what I thought was the best for me. Yet while I thought I knew what my wife to be was supposed to be like, the Lord put Shannah, the love of my life, in front of me that evening on South Beach for a very specific reason. When we met, I was living in Gainesville, attending school at the University of Florida and was in Miami for the holidays. Amazingly, Shannah was leaving for Gainesville in two days. When I asked her where she was going to be living she said she was moving into "Oakbrook Walk Apartments" precisely the same place that I was already living. - Coincidence? No; "God incidence". If you are not familiar with Gainesville, there are thousands of rental apartments and condos that students lease during semesters.

Our dating years in college were hard. We were so different in so many ways. We would break up and get back together constantly. I was immature and more interested in having a good time than my studying. Since, this was not the woman I would marry, I thought, it's okay to have her as a girlfriend for now but I will never marry Shannah. The years went by and eventually we did break up for a longer period of time. We saw each other and stayed in touch by virtue of having the same friends. I treated her poorly then (which she will never let me forget and for which I've since made up). I was immature and decided that she didn't matter. Besides, I thought I could have her back at anytime. One summer my family and I traveled to the Bahamas to fish. We were in absolute paradise and I was doing what I love to do most in life. Yet for reasons only the Lord knew at that time, I was only thinking about Shannah. Up to this point, I had convinced myself that I didn't really love her, but I did. I had convinced myself that we could never work. I kept telling myself that marrying her would be a disaster, yet for the first time I realized that I did love her. I realized that all those other differences did not matter and that I had to grow up and tell her that I did love her and that I was now mature.

As soon as I returned from Great Harbor, Bahamas, I called Shannah (I knew she would answer- this girl adored me) I invited her out to dinner to her favorite restaurant, The Rusty Pelican on Key

Biscayne, and she accepted. I wore a suit and tie because I wanted to show her that I was now mature and that I did want to be with her. She looked beautiful the night I picked her up and off we went to dinner. To my shock, she kept looking at her watch and receiving phone calls during dinner from friends. She told me that she had a boyfriend and that she wasn't really interested in me anymore. More than what she told me was the way in which she said it. She meant it, she was finally over me. I couldn't believe my ears. Did she accept my dinner invitation just so that she could close this chapter in her life? Was she just interested in having a lobster dinner and curious to see my reaction to her news? It just wasn't clear. The night ended somewhat coldly and that was it. Now I was on the other end of the relationship; I wanted her and she did not want to be with me. I became resentful but remained persistent. A few months later, Shannah's grandmother, whom she was very close to and the one true mother she has known, passed away. Beverly was a wonderful and caring woman who treated me very kindly while she was alive. When this happened Shannah reached out to me for support. I was confused and stupidly figured that the best way to have Shannah back was to treat her like I did in college. I could not believe that now that I was being nice and truly wanted a relationship with her that she had pushed me away. I did speak with her and consoled her in her loss, but I foolishly did not attend her grandmother's funeral. I still regret that to this day.

I continued to court Shannah and she continued to reject me. One special evening, my friend Andy and I went to a club on Miami Beach. That night we two bachelors who were out for a good time both danced with the women we would eventually marry. Andy met a girl that night and they instantly hit it off. They danced the whole night. Andy was never much of a dancer, but that night he was dancing as though he was Fred Astaire. Shannah came to the same club coincidentally, with a group of friends. She looked stunning and just like something out of a corny movie, we saw each other from across the dance floor and one of our favorite songs began to play. We began dancing and at one point as we danced, she looked into my eyes and whispered, "I love you." I replied and things changed in our relationship for the better from then on.

When I was 24 years old, we were married twice in two days; first by a priest and next by a Rabbi. Our marriage by the priest was kept secret to Shannah's family. Shannah's family, although Jewish in tradition does not practice their faith with any regularity. During the early years of our marriage, we did not speak of Jesus to not offend Shannah's family. I could speak of Judaism but not of what I believed about Christ. Our Jewish wedding was enormous with over 200 persons invited. Unfortunately there was a category 1 hurricane (Irene) on the day before our wedding. The idea was to have the Rabbi and the Priest together; however, the Priest was flooded in and could not make it to the wedding. Consequent to the hurricane, about 80 of our guests could not arrive. We were married by the Rabbi and our wedding reception would be indicative of our lives to come. My family is a very large, very Cuban Catholic and boisterous group, many of its members only speak Spanish. Shannah's family is Jewish, reserved and only speaks English.

Because of all these differences, I believe the common ground was drinking (a lot of it) dancing and fun. What we witnessed at our wedding was inexplicable and downright hilarious. The DJ was mixing Gloria Estefan and Hava Nagila. People that could not even speak the same language were dancing together and having a great time. If you are ever in need of a good laugh, come by our house and Shannah and I will be happy to show you the video of that hilarious night.

This is illustrative of how our families have gotten along. While there are many, many differences, they have always found a way to reach common ground. I have learned to love Shannah's family dearly and accept them as my own.

We have been married for 9 years, some years better than other, but our relationship and our understanding of each other improves everyday.

BELLA'S STORY

The birth of our first daughter Bella could have not been more joyful. We were excited as all new parents are but this was exceptionally special for two major reasons. First, my parents were still alive, in good health and would most definitely get an opportunity to know and help raise my child. Second, we were having a girl. I wanted so badly to give my mother another girl. My mother lost her first child (Carmen) when she was two days old back in Cuba, she had only boys and all of my brother's children were also boys. I was the last hope for a girl. I asked the Lord to please let me have a girl for my mother and was overjoyed to know I was going to be able to give my mother another girl.

Shannah's delivery of Bella was complicated. She and I went to the hospital one evening because she was having minor contractions. After an ultrasound it was determined that Shannah had low amniotic fluid. The doctor at the hospital instructed us to return home, have dinner, and collect our belongings and come back to be admitted. We returned to the hospital a few hours later and the next morning Shannah's labor was induced. Shannah was in labor for 13 hours and because Bella did not progress at all, it was decided to conduct a cesarean section.

Bella was born on December 12, 2002. The entire family was overjoyed with our baby girl. While the labor was not easy, Bella appeared to be healthy and normal. After 3 days in the hospital, we went home with our new bundle of joy.

Bella was a happy infant and normal by most standards. My father being a pediatrician observed keenly her development and was happy with how Bella was progressing during her early months. Around eight months of age, everything changed. Some of our friends and acquaintances also had children around Bella's age. We would sometimes get together with them and all of the babies. Shannah and I noticed that Bella did not make any attempt to roll over or try to sit up, something the other children were doing. In fact, some had already started crawling and sitting up. While I was oblivious that anything might be wrong, thinking simply that Bella was a late bloomer, Shannah who is a special education teacher and my father privately began to notice that Bella was not achieving certain important milestones in her development. In fact at this point, the back of Bella's head had started to flatten since she did little more than constantly lie on her back.

One day while Shannah attended a "mommy and me" play class with Bella, the teacher of the class approached Shannah in private. She asked Shannah if Bella had ever been given a neurological work up. She said that she noticed that Bella was far behind the other children and that it would probably be a good idea. Shannah agreed.

Shannah returned home and told me what the teacher at the class had said. My response was one of disbelief and denial. Shannah being trained as a special education teacher certainly knew what to look for and called my father to discuss the issue. My father confessed that he too had observed that Bella was not developing optimally; he suggested a neurologist who is a dear friend for an evaluation.

During the evaluation, Bella was diagnosed with global developmental delay and low muscle tone "hypotonia." He prescribed physical, occupational and speech therapy. This was the beginning of a very demanding weekly schedule of therapies for Shannah and Bella which has continued for years. By the grace of God, with the help of the physical therapy, Bella learned to sit up and crawl.

Her head returned to normal shape and her fine motor skills were improving. Her speech and language unfortunately was and still is much delayed.

In addition to the challenge of her developmental delays, Bella also began to develop a severe sleep disorder. She never slept a full night in four years and subsequently neither did we. We were desperate and tried every kind of remedy you can imagine. We tried everything from holistic supplements to medicines and even a very expensive sleep consultant. While the consultant proved to be the most effective, Bella still did not sleep a full night's sleep.

The years between Bella's diagnosis of the developmental delay up until she was about four were challenging on many fronts. Bella did not adapt well in social situations. She also had a "self regulation disorder" which meant that if she was upset, it would take her literally hours to calm down. If we were anywhere in public or at a birthday party, we would have to be ready to leave abruptly because Bella could not adjust. Also, because of her severe speech delay, Bella would get very frustrated and would whine loudly, uncontrollably and would also hit other children in her frustration of not being able to communicate. You can imagine how unwelcoming the parents of other children were to us and Bella because of this. It was hurtful to feel the weight of stares from other parents and children who would often laugh and mimic the tantrum fits that Bella would display.

Our life was very predictable, we were always home. We did not go out with Bella, we would constantly try to get her to nap or sleep and everyone was exhausted. We had Bella tested for autism by a renowned neurologist who specialized in this area. Fortunately, it was determined that Bella did not suffer from autism, and that all therapies should continue. It was a very frustrating time, because nothing specifically could be found with Bella other than that she was delayed. Many, including our own family, dismissed or downplayed that she had anything wrong with her other than bad behavior, bad parenting and being a late bloomer. We would not attend family gatherings in fear of the inevitable debacle Shannah and I knowingly expected. The few times we went out in public during those years, people would be so mean. If we went to a restaurant people would make comments about us. It was terrible. One evening at a restaurant for dinner, we even had someone come over to us and say, "You really need to learn how to parent your child." People can sometimes be so cruel and unkind when they lack understanding or view what differs from their norms.

In 2005, our second daughter Rayna was born. This was a big surprise as our marriage was in the worst shape ever. Of course, if it were not for these surprises, I suppose that half of us would not be here. We were in complete shock that Shannah was pregnant. What a funny sense of humor God has. We could not believe that we were now going to have another baby, given all the work that raising Bella was. Yet, Rayna was and continues to be such an amazing little girl and such a blessing for all of us.

Our life with Bella continued to be challenging. In 2005 I had to travel to Puerto Rico as I had been promoted and I was going to meet with my employees there one final time. We decided to take the trip as a family. At the time, Bella was three and a half and Rayna was one and a half. Shannah and I had shared some apprehension before embarking on the trip. After all, cooped up in an airplane for several hours with two small children has never been known to be a parent's favorite past time. And knowing Bella's challenges when outside of her familiar surroundings could prove to be disastrous. On the flight, Bella had such an attack of not being able to regulate herself that people would give us dirty looks and we even had one passenger say "I don't know how much more I can take of this." Bella was hysterical, she was kicking the seat in front of her and banging her head, all the while screaming. When the plane finally landed Shannah was crying, the plane was full and people from the airport even entered the plane to see what was the matter. As they made their way towards our aisle against the flow of passengers that were exiting the plane, Bella was getting even worse. Every person passing by our aisle as we were stuck in the middle would give us dirty looks or make comments under their breath. Puerto Rico is extremely hot in the summer and this day was no exception. The heat combined with the smell of jet fuel added to the discomfort of this adventure. In my desperation, seeing my daughter in dismay and my wife suffering from frustration and embarrassment, within seconds it all came to a boil and in an effort to alleviate the situation I stood up and said "people, please she has autism, please leave us alone." As I stated before, Bella, thank God, does not have autism, but it is the only thing I could think of to make people understand that this was not just a bratty, unruly kid. I felt so humiliated and berated by the lack of compassion and empathy that it reminded me of what an outcast of our society must at times experience. In that particular situation, we were the outcasts!

When we finally got to our hotel we were so distraught, that Shannah told me, she refused to go back to Miami on a plane. Who could blame her? None of us wanted to relive the horrible experience we had just endured. We explored taking a ship back home. I called American Airlines and explained Bella's situation and how "shell shocked" we were. They informed me that in accordance with the Americans with Disabilities Act (ADA) they would most certainly give us seats near the bulkhead which would make Bella more comfortable. The problem however is that only one parent could sit with her. After considering different options, we felt there would be no faster way back than getting on another airplane. We decided that Bella might be more agitated sitting with only one of us, so we returned to Miami on a flight and sat together. With our doctor's approval, we gave Bella three times the appropriate dose of Benadryl and took an evening flight, in hopes she would sleep. Thank God, Bella had a much better flight, but did not fall asleep despite our efforts.

The terrible experience on the plane and the other social nightmares we experienced are hard to describe. As stated before even members of our family dismissed what we were going through. They would tell us stories such as "my mother had a cousin who was delayed, in fact he didn't speak until he was 8 years old, and he eventually became a genius and a millionaire." Those types of comments did not help, we knew there was something wrong with Bella, but because there was nothing physically wrong with her, people assumed she was just a brat with bad parenting. Sometimes the people that hurt you most are also the ones that love you most. I know that sounds like such a cliché, but it is true.

Later in 2006, one of her doctors reluctantly ordered an MRI of Bella's brain because Shannah and I insisted. The MRI revealed that Bella had a condition called Periventricular Leukomalacia. These are strokes in the white matter of her brain which are caused by low oxygen or hypoxia at birth.

While Periventricular Leukomalacia (PVL) is not by any means something to hope for, we at least knew what was at the root of the issue. The plan was to ramp up her therapies and to get out of complete denial that Bella was just a late bloomer with a little delay. Incredibly, now with this MRI as proof so many around us became understanding, particularly our own family members. Now it was for real, it wasn't just bad parenting or a little delay, there really was something not quite right with Bella. While it felt good for Shannah and me to begin to hear words of understanding, it certainly did not erase the years we had experienced of trouble and the continued sleepless nights we were living. It also gave us some degree of concern for the future. Would there be any long-term effects? Would Bella always have behavioral and comprehension problems? Would she ever catch up to her peers?

While life was not easy during these years, we felt fortunate. Who better to handle a situation like this? Our family was very well prepared, with a special education teacher as a mother and a loving and renowned pediatrician as a grandfather. Who better than us to tackle this? We continued to face the issue head on and continued the course with therapy and special education class at the local public school for Bella.

For many months life improved for our family. Bella was attending two schools, in the morning she would attend special education and in the afternoon she would attend a typical setting classroom at the Jewish Community Center in Miami. In addition, we had therapists come to our home everyday. We also received help from a great non profit organization in Miami called the Friendship Circle. This is an organization where teenagers volunteer to go to the homes of special needs children like Bella and play with them. In short, while our life was very hectic with an activity packed week for both Bella and Shannah, we had a steady routine. Bella even began to sleep better; although she still did not sleep through the night, it was better. Our family and close friends even became more understanding and everyone would come to our house, understanding that it was not easy for us to get out. We had learned to accept and adapt to doing things in new ways.

I was very involved with my work, but thankfully my position is one where I have great flexibility and work from home. The downside to my position is that I had to travel extensively. This was hard for all of us but in particular for Shannah who had to "hold down the fort" alone. While I was making a very good living by the age of 28, there was obviously, because of the travel, some sacrifice. I often considered taking a job in Miami so that I would not have to travel, yet I would be working everyday from morning until night in an office and could not have the flexibility I had of occasionally going to therapy with Bella and Shannah or watching Rayna when I was working from home. Besides, I made very good money and I needed it. Bella's co pays and optional therapies were and continue to be, quite expensive. Nonetheless, things were going well and we were thankful to God that we could handle the situation, particularly because the level of PVL that Bella has is extremely mild. A large percentage of the children diagnosed with PVL end up with Cerebral Palsy, in a wheel chair and experience a multitude of health and neurological problems. On a scale from 1-10 in severity, thank God Bella's condition was a 1. Things could *always* be worse, and we felt very fortunate that this was a mild impediment on the grand scale of things.

SHE WILL WALK OUT OF HERE!

After the short flight from Orlando, I arrived at Miami Children's Hospital emergency room and was greeted by my friend Jose. Jose and I have been close friends since our childhood. We went to school together and we have shared many good times together and have known each other since third grade. Fortunately, after receiving my phone call when I was in the Orlando airport, he decided to end his lunch meeting and head to the hospital to accompany Shannah and Bella; what a blessing.

When I arrived, I found an exhausted Bella and Shannah. Shannah explained to me that Bella had not slept the night before. She was up all-night and was tripping and falling as she walked. In the morning she could not stand.

Imagine hearing this, I could not believe the scene before me. I was in disbelief and tried tickling Bella's thighs; nothing, she couldn't move them. Bella could not walk. She was incoherent, tired and very, very cranky especially after spending hours in the hospital. Realizing that Bella was paralyzed gave me such a sense of helplessness. I so wanted her to get up and walk, and yet there didn't appear there was anything that I could do. While I was scared, I did my best to assure Shannah that all would be ok. The lumbar puncture that evening, did in fact confirm a diagnosis of Gillian Barre Syndrome. The memories of my dad's illness came flooding back to me. My dad had made a remarkable recovery, and this provided some degree of comfort. I figured that if my dad had recovered so well and so quickly; a young child should fare even better. I prayed alone in the hallway and asked God to please be with us and to restore Bella. *Why God, Why me?*

Bella was transferred to the Pediatric Intensive Care Unit (PICU) to begin what was now the standard therapy for Gillian Barre Syndrome (GBS); high dose Immunoglobulin (IVIG) for 5 days. In 2007, contrary to 1995, when my father had GBS, it was now known that high dose immunoglobulin was the best treatment for GBS. The reason for the transfer was because the treatment has been known to cause severe side effects including death, so it is very important that the first doses are given under very close supervision. The first night in the PICU was tough. We were in semi-isolation in that, Bella was secluded in a corner of the unit but was part of the general population of the other patients. Everywhere around us were tubes, machinery, monitors, and many nurses who were very busy. At times it seemed like a human ant farm with people running back and forth and constantly tending to these children's need. The mental images of the first night were quite disturbing. There were two children that went into cardiac arrest and died that night right before my very eyes. Fortunately Bella was asleep. As I sat there watching the nurses and doctors trying to save these little children, I beheld the reality around me; here I was, with my daughter paralyzed lying next to me. *Why God?* Why am I here? What have I done? Why Bella? *Why me?* My heart went out to the parents and families of these children. Their little loved ones had lost their fight. Now they would have to deal with making funeral arrangements and such. It is such a somber event and tragedy for any family. Children are our most precious possessions. No child should ever have to suffer.

Bella's first night was thankfully without event. Because of this, she was moved the following day to the neurology floor, given that she tolerated the first night of immunoglobulin (IVIG) with no side effects.

For the following three days, Bella continued her IVIG treatment; thankfully, she continued without any side effects. She was paralyzed and everyone dealt with the consequences of her not being able to move; including going to the bathroom which took on an incredible new challenge of carrying and cleaning Bella every time she went, which now was at times unannounced because she could not feel her bowels.

Those days were difficult for everyone. We had begun to realize that Bella would not walk immediately however the research on GBS was that eventually nearly all patients caught as early and treated as aggressively as Bella did, do eventually walk. Perhaps days, weeks or months later, but it was known that IVIG treatment was the right way to go. I was the optimistic cheerleader and kept telling Shannah, "She is going to walk out of here." I told Shannah, "On day five of the treatment, her legs will start working again and she is going to walk out of here!" I needed to be strong and lift Shannah up. She couldn't see me crumble, but there were many tears that I shed in the silence of lonely drives to and from the hospital. I often think as I walk the hallways of hospitals, how many tears have been shed by others as they too have walked the corridors of despair. If the walls of any hospital could speak, the stories must be filled with a great deal of suffering, agony, desperation, and pain.

Unfortunately, Bella was not improving. In fact, her paralysis seemed to be getting worse. She went from not being able to move her legs to not being able to wiggle her toes. I had to accept the fact that Bella was not going to walk out of there. I started to fall into a depression realizing that our lives going home were going to be very different. She was going to go home in a wheel chair. My little girl, my little treasure was going to be confined to a wheelchair and life had not prepared me for this. So many images of her jumping, running, and playing in our backyard seemed to flash before me. Her swing set in the yard that she loved so much, would now stand as a reminder of what she would no longer be able to do. I stepped out to the hallway, with my stomach turning inside me. I had a cold sweat dripping down my neck and with sadness and disappointment in my voice, I made a phone call. I called my neighbor Ronnie who is very handy and asked him to start making some wheel chair ramps for our home. Ronnie was very helpful and open to helping in anyway. I was destroyed, I had been hopeful that she would recover, but sadly that was not the case. I had to accept reality.

On day four of the IVIG, her neurologist and physical therapist suggested that Bella visit the physical therapy gym at the hospital so that she could familiarize herself with the surroundings. Up until this point, we could tell that Bella's legs and toes could not move, but we had no idea how bad the paralysis really was. We went down to the ground floor at Miami Children's Hospital and entered the gym. Once we put Bella on the mat, everyone present was in shock as we immediately realized that Bella's paralysis was much worse than anyone had imagined. We came to see that Bella could not sit up. She would fall face forward onto the mat. She had no abdominal muscles; she had no leg muscles and would drag herself with her arms across the floor. She was as a paraplegic and she was just as terrified as were all of us. There are certain memories that are etched into your mind forever and sadly, this was going to be one that I will take with me to my grave. My stomach tightened, my heart raced, I could not believe the horror of what I was watching. It was almost like watching a film in slow motion. Every inch of her hands and arms were clawing at the mat in an effort to move. It was one of the most heart-wrenching scenes that any parent should ever have to witness. She appeared like a little animal that has been hit by car and had her legs broken. Our Bella was helpless! Inside, I was screaming *Why God?* Nonetheless, I somehow kept my cool on the outside. Shannah's emotions got the best of her and she began to cry. We picked Bella up off the floor and took her back to her room and laid her in bed.

What a disappointment I thought "My God will she really ever walk again?" This is much worse than we thought! Because of what was observed at the gym and the fact that she appeared not to be progressing, it was decided to schedule an MRI of Bella's spine the following day.

THE WORST DAY

Shannah had spent the night with Bella in the hospital and I had gone home to get some much needed sleep and to spend some time with Rayna. The following morning, Shannah had taken Bella to anesthesia and Bella was sedated for her MRI. I arrived at Miami Children's Hospital at around 9:15AM. When I arrived, I saw my father and Shannah sitting in the hospital lobby together. I sat next to Shannah in one of the many brightly colored chairs; that you would expect to see in a children's hospital. While we were not in a happy mood by any means, we were at least content to finally be going home and starting our new life with Bella in a wheel chair and what we knew would be intense days of physical therapy. We wanted to go home, we wanted to be together with Rayna and although the situation was bad, we were ready for home. After conversing for about three minutes with Shannah and my father, I was paged over a loud speaker to radiology. I figured that I was being called to sign one of the many parental waivers I had already been accustomed to sign for every procedure Bella had been subjected to thus far. Unfortunately, this call was very different and it was meant to call my attention in a very different manner.

I arose from my seat and began to walk toward the radiology reception. When I got up, I noticed that my father also got up. He was walking with me and now Shannah was sitting alone in the lobby. As soon as my father and I turned the corner and were out of Shannah's sight, my father turned to me. He was crying, I had never seen my father cry before. He said "I have something to tell you, but I don't know how to tell you this. Bella's MRI shows that she does not have GBS, she has a tumor around her spinal cord, she has what we believe to be cancer."

I froze, I could not believe what I was hearing, but seeing my father with tears in his eyes made the moment unforgettable. At that very moment, the words my father had just uttered to me seemed surreal. Cancer? My child was just fine with nothing but a little upset stomach and now she has cancer? How could this be happening? All the background noise in the hallway of the hospital seemed to come to a standstill. For a moment, all I could hear was the beating of my heart, which was pounding like a drum in my chest. I said "what do we do?" At that moment the Chief of Pediatrics of the hospital, Dr. Deise Granado-Villar who is a dear friend and practically like family walked towards us. She and the entire team of physicians had already been studying the results of Bella's MRI. In fact there were no papers for me to sign, my father staged the whole pager thing so that he could speak to me alone. He had known the results of the MRI, had been sitting next to Shannah and didn't know what to do. As Dr. Granado-Villar, my father and I stood there in disbelief, we all could not imagine delivering the news to Shannah, but we had to. Dr. Granado-Villar came with us and said, "I will talk to her." My father and I were in no condition to deliver this news. As the three of us walked toward Shannah to address her, I felt as though it were an out of body experience. It was like watching a movie. The short hallway seemed to be unending. With each step it seemed like the hallway was extending itself and I could not get to her. Here I was walking and trying to maintain my composure trying not to alert her with my emotion or body language from a distance.

Dr. Granado-Villar began to deliver the news. Shannah stood up and said," I'm sorry, could you repeat that?" Dr. Granado-Villar said, "The MRI shows that Bella has a mass wrapped around her spine." Shannah began to slowly fall back into her chair in utter shock. "Are you listening to what I am saying?" Dr. Granado-Villar asked. "We must take her to spinal surgery right away." Shannah answered "No, I am not listening. Are you telling me that Bella has cancer?" She answered "Yes". Shannah whispered, "Please get me some medication, I can't breathe, I think I'm having a panic attack." Dr. Granado-Villar said, "Okay, but then we must go see the Neurosurgeon, he is waiting to speak with us." Dr. Granado-Villar immediately ran to the pharmacy wrote a prescription for Xanax, and brought it to Shannah.

When we arrived at the Neurosurgeons' office in the medical arts building, the door just opened and we sat in an exam room waiting for him to enter. He greeted us and showed us the MRI of Bella's spine, which showed a Mass wrapped around her spinal cord and vertebrae. He explained that he would enter through the back and remove as much as he could to free the spinal cord. He said that there would be much that he would not be able to remove as most of the Mass was in front of the cord and not in a place he felt comfortable cutting because of possible further damage to the spine. We asked him if Bella would ever walk again. He said "most likely not. She is not walking now and usually what you cannot do prior to this kind of surgery, you will not be able to do afterward." We asked him in our desperation, "Will she live?" He said, "It will certainly help." We asked him a few other questions about the surgery and he reassured us kindly by saying "if this were my daughter this is what I would do." He said he would be ready for surgery in an hour and that he would see us in the PICU.

We walked back down to the hospital lobby in complete shock and disbelief. This felt surreal. We must be dreaming and it is a nightmare that we need to wake up from. We walked crying and with blank stares on our faces. How could this be? How did she develop a tumor? We were supposed to be going home and now this? Shannah and I found a corner in the lobby and began to call family and friends. The first person I called was my brother Ralph in Orlando. As I mentioned prior, Ralph is my older middle brother, he is more like a second father to me and like my father, my best friend. Once again, I was overcome by emotion. When he answered the phone, I could barely speak. I was able to mumble: "They found a tumor". My brother reacted with a loud *"What?"* He had heard what I had said, but just couldn't register it at that moment. I repeated it and Ralph began to cry hysterically. He, my sister-in-law, Kim, who is Bella's Godmother, and their son Christian, were driving on a causeway at that very moment and I could hear Kim in the background telling him to pullover. I told Ralph that Bella had a tumor on her spinal cord and that she would be going into a surgery that would last about 3 hours. With absolute fear in my voice, flooded with tears, I told him that I desperately needed him to fly back to Miami. Ralph had just been in Miami with us and left on Sunday. He, Kim, and Christian had just been here for several days when Bella was first diagnosed with GBS. Here it was Tuesday morning and I needed him back! As Ralph often says, "This is the first time the earth stood still." I told him that if Bella didn't make it through surgery I don't know what I would do and I needed him. I feared that Bella was going to die during the surgery. Ralph and Kim were not at home; they were an hour away securing their beach condo in New Smyrna Beach from a storm that was approaching that area. He said he would get on the first flight possible. Shannah and I made some other phone calls and then were told that Bella would be moving to the PICU.

At this point, the team's plan was to take Bella from the MRI suite where she was already under anesthesia and prepare her for deeper sedation and spinal surgery. When Dr. Granado-Villar, my father, Shannah and I entered the PICU, it was a chaotic scene.

By now many of the hospital employees who love my father so dearly and worked with him for so many years when he was chief of staff, had learned of what was happening to Bella. The PICU was packed full of those caring for Bella and other hospital employees who were there for support. The tension in the room was extremely high and there was a squad of nurses and physicians swarming over Bella, who was unconscious and being ventilated. I had already seen Bella intubated twice that week, but this was entirely different. They were hooking her up to multiple IVs and other devices. People were extremely nervous, emotions high and some began yelling, "Treat this little girl as though she was my daughter, you save her life!"

Indeed the mental images I have of this are the worst moments of my life. My precious daughter, who one week ago was at summer camp swimming, was laying there unconscious with tubes and apparatus hanging from every inch of her body. I felt every emotion from fear, terror, anxiety, despair and anger, but mostly complete disbelief and shock. Shannah suddenly become overwhelmed by the whole situation and thought she might faint. Some of us, including a PICU physician, brought her a chair and began to comfort and console her. It was terrible, as if the ground itself opened up and was about to swallow us. Our world as we knew it was no more.

Before Bella was to go into surgery, I had asked a priest to come and anoint her. The priest, who was the Chaplain at the hospital, arrived immediately. He and I stood there trying to lay hands on Bella, but because of so many people working rapidly over her we were not able to physically touch her. I pleaded with the young charge nurse to allow us a few minutes to pray over Bella, but it was an emergency. Finally, when she was stable and all of the machines were working correctly, we were granted our 2 minutes to pray over Bella. When the priest prayed over Bella and anointed her forehead with oil to give her the sacrament of anointing of the sick, we felt a moment of temporary peace. Immediately after, however, reality struck. We were informed that Bella was needed right away in the operating room (OR). An entourage of people, including Shannah and I, pushed her stretcher as she laid there unconscious towards the OR. At the door of the sterile area which we could not enter, I blessed and prayed over my little angel. I asked God to be with her and save her. I asked God to give her medical team expedience and precise diligence in their work to save my daughter, and just like that she went off to surgery.

At this point various members of our large family began to arrive at the hospital. We essentially took over the surgical waiting room and as more friends and family began to arrive, our group overflowed into the hallway. I was pacing the hallway and desperately awaiting the arrival of my brother Ralph. While I was being as strong as I could be for Shannah, inside I was a wreck, my stomach was turning, my palms were sweating and I had a persistent cold sweat around my neck. I needed someone, and that someone was and continues to be Ralph. As I was pacing the hallway in front of the OR alone, I saw the Neurosurgeon enter. I stopped him and told him that I had asked God to bless his hands.

A short while after the surgery began; my father was paged by pathology. I went with him and left Shannah upstairs with our family, friends, hospital employees and others. I followed my father to the pathology department. There I met the Pathologist who would be studying the tissue being removed from Bella to determine the type of tumor it was. I also met another Pathologist who was called in as a favor to also give his opinion. It was amazing to see so many people reach out to help us in such a desperate time out of the goodness of their hearts.

Up until this point, many physicians who are friends of our family, including Bella's primary pediatrician, all reassured us that the tumor looked like a lymphoma on the MRI. They told us that if you were going to have pediatric cancer, Lymphoma would be the best scenario as in most cases it was now, with modern medicine, highly treatable. It had to be a Lymphoma and everybody was betting on that. Shannah and I were researching Lymphoma on the internet using my Blackberry. We were already researching treatment options, survival chances and the like. We read how many advances had been made in treating Lymphoma. We too felt optimistic that it was Lymphoma. Can you imagine hoping for Lymphoma? What a terrible scenario it was. At moments such as these, you are willing to negotiate in exchange for something other than a worst case scenario.

As the Neurosurgeon cut pieces of the tumor from Bella's spine, those tissues were being delivered to the resection room, where my father and I were. I actually saw pieces of Bella's bloody tissue. I saw with my own eyes, the cancer that had invaded her body and caused her to be paralyzed. The pathologists worked quickly and were able to get what is called a "frozen section" or small piece of tissue on a slide to view under a microscope. The group in the room, including the Director of Oncology all moved to the microscope room. They placed the slide under a large microscope which had multiple eyelids, also known as teaching tube, so that many people could observe the same image at the same time. At this point, the first Pathologist began analyzing the tissue. He concluded that the tumor was called a Small Round Blue Cell Tumor. He certainly ruled out Lymphoma and felt that it was most likely a tumor called Neuroblastoma. The second pathologist followed, speaking aloud as he also made his observations. He concluded the same, he felt it was Neuroblastoma. I could immediately tell by everyone's reaction in the room that this was worse than what they were originally anticipating. Certainly they were not as optimistic as when they believed it was Lymphoma. Human beings have strong non-verbal communications that can yield a great deal in times such as these. Nonetheless, I remember Dr. Granado-Villar turning to me and saying "Its okay Raymond, there are three types of round blue cell tumors which it could have been, Rhabdomyosarcoma is the worst, and Thank God it is not that. Neuroblastoma is not good, but it is treatable and Bella can have a bone marrow or stem cell transplant." The tissue was automatically being sent overnight to the Reference Laboratory for confirmation and for further specialized testing.

I returned upstairs to where Shannah and the rest of the group were. As my father and I walked, we decided not to say anything about what had just occurred in pathology. We were so optimistic that it was a Lymphoma that we wanted to wait until the Reference Laboratory responded before any further speculation. As I stood next to Shannah, I did not tell her where I had been nor what I had seen and heard. We stood together in the hallway waiting for the Neurosurgeon to come out of surgery and give us a report. As we stood there together, Bella's primary pediatrician who had heard that the tumor was believed to be Neuroblastoma approached us assuming Shannah knew. With best intentions, she assured us that while the news was not good, today Nueroblastoma could be treated and that she had two patients with Neuroblastoma who had previously been treated at Memorial Sloan Kettering Cancer Center in New York and survived. Shannah was shell-shocked and asked me if I knew what she was talking about, of course I told her the truth about what had transpired. She immediately began researching Nueroblastoma and learned how much more devastating and aggressive it was compared to Lymphoma. The chances of survival are much worse and the treatments much more invasive and aggressive.

Finally, my brother Ralph arrived. The director of the laboratory at the hospital had picked him up at the airport as a favor to our family. His arrival immediately provided some comfort for all of us. He walked out of the elevator and gave me a strong embrace. The news had hit him hard, for he loves us and our children almost as if they were his own. Shortly thereafter, the Neurosurgeon exited the operating room, after four hours. He addressed a large portion of our family which was now in the hallway. He said that he was only able to remove a small portion of the tumor from the back, but he was able to ease some pressure on the spinal cord. He said that Bella was doing well, but unfortunately, given that the tumor was around the spinal cord, around and in the vertebrae and to his disappointment in between the discs, he was certain she would never walk again.

The news was oddly bittersweet. While it was devastating to hear that he felt certain Bella would never walk again, we were glad she was out of surgery and doing well. Our large group stayed with us for a long time and many brought food and drinks for everyone as they showed their support. In an effort to stay optimistic, I began telling everyone that once the surgery was over, Bella's legs would begin to work and that "she would walk out of this hospital!" My oldest nephew Alex also encouraged my optimism by echoing my sentiment to everyone. We were informed that Bella was going to be staying in the PICU overnight once they were finished in the operating room. Shannah and I decided that I would stay with her in the PICU as only one person is allowed to be with the patient. There are no beds or recliners for family in the PICU, only chairs. Thank God I can function with very little sleep.

That night in the PICU was the longest of my life. My daughter laid there unconscious and paralyzed. Her nurse would assess her every hour, including pinching and tickling her toes to see if they would move, unfortunately they would not. I was desperate, I was angry and I wanted to see those legs move. When the nurse wasn't looking I would pinch her little toe as hard as I could in hopes that she would respond, she wouldn't. If you've never spent a night in a pediatric ICU, you should consider yourself blessed. It is one of the saddest places you could ever visit. No ICU is ever pleasant, but there is something even more disturbing about seeing children suffer. There were children of all ages. Some children who were just a few hours old and others who were in the pre-teen years. The common denominator they shared, was affliction and suffering.

During this time in the PICU is when the Lord began showing me the first of many signs to come. No one is allowed to talk on cell phones in the ICU as they can interfere with the equipment, however my Blackberry was receiving e-mail. I began to receive message after message from colleagues, friends and those that I didn't know, telling me that they were with me in spirit, they were praying and to remain strong. While I was alone with Bella, all those wonderful people were reaching out to me the only way they could. Indeed they were with me that night, more than they can ever imagine.

I did not sleep at all that night, I kept squeezing Bella's toes and around 6:00AM, her Neurosurgeon came to see her in the PICU. He said she looked well and that her incision was healing well. He informed me that barring any complications, she would be returning back to her room on the Neurology floor later that day. Shannah and Ralph had spent the night trying to get some sleep in the hospital room on the Neurology floor and came to replace me in the PICU around 7: OO AM. I went home, cried and got some much needed rest. It had been a long, exhausting and trying night.

Around noon, Bella went back to her room on the Neurology floor where she was allowed to recover from her surgery in her room. She was on morphine and was in and out of consciousness throughout the day and night. The number of visitors was so incredible that the hospital assigned an office and lounge down the hall from Bella's room as a gathering place for us. The administration of the hospital catered lunch for our family and our guests out of respect for my father and our family. They were so very gracious. We felt so thankful for the special attention and graciousness that was being demonstrated to us. We were well aware that this does not just happen to the average patient. Our treatment was the result of love, respect, and admiration on behalf of my father. Even the CEO of the hospital came to personally visit Bella in the PICU and was greeted by Ralph and Shannah, since they were the ones on duty at the time. The mood was sad, but those that visited did their best to cheer us up. There were so many visitors it was overwhelming. Finally, the nurses put a sign on the door saying that there were no more visitors allowed in the room and directed them to the office where our family and visitors could go. This was a great relief, as Shannah, myself and Bella no longer had the energy to welcome visitors. People meant well, but it was just too much too soon!

Two days later, Bella had what is called a PET scan, which is a test where a contrast is injected into the body to see if the cancer had spread (metastasized) to other areas. The results were, that in addition to the spine, Bella had tumors in her right jaw, left shoulder, left rib, left hip, left knee, right foot and left hand. She was invaded! Her precious little body had been incubating these tumors for God knows how long.

I later learned that my father had already had the official diagnosis by the Reference Laboratory that evening. He had called my father- in- law Myles and delivered the devastating news that Shannah and I would officially learn the next day, on Friday. Ralph had managed to pry the information out of my dad, and under a solemn vow had promised he would not breathe a word to us until the meeting with the oncologist. My brother had managed to put on a great poker face, because although Shannah suspected he knew something, Ralph managed to play it cool. He kept his promise to my father. I am sure he silently suffered that evening, because he knew how serious the situation really was.

"It's Worth a Shot"

Anyone who has experienced occasional insomnia knows that the night can seem like an endless journey of tossing and turning. No matter how many sheep you count, no matter how many peaceful images you place in your mind; the night drags on until the first rays of sunlight begins to break the darkness of night. On Friday morning July 20th, 2007, Shannah and I met with Dr. Enrique Escalon the Director of Oncology of Miami Children's Hospital. I have known Enrique virtually all of my life. He too has a profound appreciation for my father and our family and was also affected by all that was happening. He certainly composed himself and did his best to deliver the news to Shannah and I in the best way he could. We had both decided that in addition to my father, we needed to have both Myles and Ralph present during the meeting. So, gathered in the private office, we came together to anxiously get the tough answers we had been anticipating. He told us that the Reference Laboratory had confirmed that unfortunately Bella's tumor was not Neuroblastoma, but Rhabdomyosarcoma. Precisely the tumor we were praying it would NOT be. Of the two subtypes, Bella had Alveolar Rhabdomyosarcoma, which is the more aggressive of the two. He told us that Bella's official diagnosis was stage 4, group 4, Metastatic Alveolar Rhabdomyosarcoma. He also told us that this unfortunately put Bella in the worst prognostic setting possible.

Ralph says this is the second time the earth stood still. By that, he means that when shocking and unexpected news is delivered before its time, it is almost as if time stands still and the world momentarily stops rotating on it's axis. Everything around you just stops and begins to come back in slow motion. Shannah and I faced the reality before us; our precious daughter who had been running and living a seemingly normal life ten days prior was now paralyzed and would most likely die. Before our meeting had ended, Shannah stood up and in a daze, walked out of the meeting and into the hospital hallway. She was crying profusely and her dad went after her and convinced her to come back in. Dr. Escalon would not give us a time frame as to how long she would live, but simply said "it's not good." The good news was that there was an experimental but very aggressive treatment protocol for this type of tumor and he suggested we begin treatment immediately. We asked him how long the treatment would be. He said it would be 54 weeks of chemotherapy and radiation. We asked him if it was even worth putting her through the hell of chemo and radiation if she was going to die anyways, he said "It's worth a shot." We were speechless. How on Earth could we deal with this for a year? The news was devastating. It seemed like our whole world had come crashing down upon us. Here we were, a young couple having to deal with a situation that seemed far beyond what we were prepared to handle. We are not supposed to be going through this! We are just young people and death is for the elderly, not the young. Dear Lord, why oh why have you forsaken us? *Why me?*

The official consent meeting ended in about an hour. Dr. Escalon informed me that there would be a series of papers I had to sign and that Bella would be moving from the Neurology floor to the Oncology floor to begin chemotherapy that same day.

I emerged from the room surprised that I was not crying and was calm and wanted to be alone. I now realized the total picture before me and had accepted that Bella would soon die. I called Andy; he immediately wanted to know what the doctor had said as he had been anxiously awaiting news from me. I composed myself and said, "Here is the deal, Bella is paralyzed and she is going to die." I cried, hung up the phone and felt completely alone.

About half an hour later, my boss, Sheri Jepsen and two of my colleagues, the same two that dropped me at the airport in Orlando, Shari Mitchell from Orlando and Cliff Jones from New Orleans arrived at the hospital. When they arrived we were outside the hospital with Bella on my lap as I sat in her wheel chair. Shannah and I figured it would be a good idea to let Bella get some fresh air before we began the hell we were about to embark on. In many ways, the arrival of my co-workers could not have come at a worse time. After all, I had just had one of the most emotionally intense meetings of my life and now I felt as if I would need to entertain my visitors. I was in no mood to play host. Little did I know that they would be the shoulders that would carry me and that I would be crying upon in just a little while. They followed us up to Bella's new room and then I spent some time with them alone. I have never felt so helpless. Among my peers I always strived to appear under control, I always wanted to be a strong leader and yet here I was sobbing uncontrollably as I hugged Sheri and both of my friends. There was no way I could control my emotions, so I let my pride go and I just cried and cried. It was nice to see them although I knew they also felt powerless. Now years later, they are still my good friends.

At anytime in my life prior to this, if you would have asked me if I had a relationship with Christ, I would have automatically answered "Yes!" After all, I attended a Catholic elementary school and high school. I earned my master's degree in business management from Oral Roberts University, one of the largest Christian Universities in the world. I was active as a youth minister in my teenage years and studied theology as an adult. Despite all of this and my supposed faith, in the moment that I should have turned to Christ the most, I felt as though I had nothing. I was destroyed. While I tried not to cry in front of Shannah, I would cry in the hallways, in the cafeteria, in front of strangers, and at night. I was truly lost and in the dark.

Because my father knew Bella's official diagnosis prior to any of us, he had begun feverishly searching for experts in the United States in Rhabdomyosarcoma. Before Bella was given any chemotherapy, the oncology team at Miami Children's Hospital hypothesized with breaking the protocol which called for chemotherapy first and no radiation until week 20 to perhaps give her radiation first, directly to the spine in order to free her legs from paralysis. In my father's search he found Dr. Paul Meyers, a sarcoma expert at the Memorial Sloan Kettering Cancer Center in New York, and had called him the day before the official diagnosis to speak with him in general terms about Bella.

As the team at Miami Children's Hospital and the radiation team at the University of Miami toyed with the idea of doing radiation first, my father desperately wished to get the opinion of Dr. Meyers before doing anything. As we waited, Dr. Meyers from New York called my father on his cell phone. My father began to explain Bella's case in general terms and suddenly much to my father's surprise, Dr. Meyers began to speak in Spanish. He explained that he spoke Spanish because his wife was originally from an island off the coast of Honduras called Roatan. It just so happens that one of my father's students who is very dear to our family lives and works in Roatan. Her name is Dr. Jaclyn Wood. In fact, one of my earliest projects as I began my professional career was equipping Dr. Wood's Medical Center with all of the medical equipment it contains today. My father asked Dr. Meyers what his wife's maiden name was and he answered "Wood." It turns out that Dr. Meyer's wife and Dr. Wood are cousins. Dr. Meyers was surprised when my father explained our family relationship with Dr. Wood and offered to help us in any way he could. He explained to my father that we should not do radiation first and should most definitely proceed with chemotherapy per the protocol.

A few hours later, Bella began her first round of chemotherapy; it was terrible. Bella changed colors several times before our eyes, she was sweating profusely, and she was trembling. She looked at me and said in her little voice "Daddy? Daddy?" It scared me so, that I thought she may be having an allergic reaction to the chemo. What if she goes into anaphylactic shock? I barked at Ralph to go out to the nurse's station and immediately get help! Within seconds, there was an army of both nurses and physicians in the room tending to Bella. You can imagine the trauma that Bella experienced at seeing this army of people coming upon her. It turned out that she was not having any allergic reaction, it was only the normal response to chemotherapy, it was horrible. I thought to myself, "there is no way I can take a year of this, God please, where are you? *"Why me?"*

THE MIRACLE BEGINS

Right after Bella finished her first round of chemo, I received a phone call that would change my life. I stepped out into the hospital hallway to receive a call from my dear friend Tim Downing who had attended Oral Roberts University with me in the graduate business program. Tim is younger than I am, and while we became friends in school, we were from separate worlds. He was an associate pastor in a church in his hometown of Paul's Valley, Oklahoma. He is a humble, incredibly bright and blessed man who also worked in real estate development. He is someone I have a tremendous amount of respect for. Tim knew what was happening with Bella and asked me a simple question, "How are you doing?" I said "I'm disappointed in myself, I know that the only person that can save Bella is God, I know that I am supposed to hand this entirely up to Him and yet, I'm not doing that. I am destroyed, I am depressed, I am crying in public, I don't know what to do!" It is then that I know that Tim spoke an inspired "word of knowledge" to me. (1 Corinthians 12:8) I have heard theologians at Oral Roberts University comment on this gift from the Holy Spirit before. The beauty of it is that we all have the gift of a "word of knowledge" and often times when we speak a message of knowledge to someone, we don't even realize that what we are about to say is inspired by God. The message we deliver to the person is something so profound that at the very moment it is spoken, it changes the way that person is thinking, feeling, and ultimately is going to act. In his thick slow and comforting southern accent, Tim proceeded to speak the following words to me; words I will never forget.

"You know Raymond, Bella has been under attack since before she was even born. She was born with those strokes in the white matter of her brain. She had difficulty learning to walk, yet overcame it, she has had difficulty learning to speak, yet she has been improving tremendously, she has had different types of developmental delays and yet she has been improving constantly. Now, she has had everything and the kitchen sink thrown at her so that she doesn't live. The question you have to ask yourself is what wonderful and miraculous things does God have planned for Bella to do for others that she has been attacked since before she was even born. What you have to do to counter this attack is not only pray for your daughter, you must build an army of people in prayer, an army of people who have perhaps been away from their faith, an army of people that are perhaps of different faiths, an army of people that perhaps have never prayed, but that is what you must do to be on the offensive of this attack."

When I hung up with Tim, I felt different. I felt that I had to do something and would no longer just feel sorry for myself. The Holy Spirit had spoken to me through Tim and the time was now for action. I felt that Tim was one of many instruments that God was using to bring me His message. I began to pray fervently and I surrendered. In my prayer I felt the Lord inspire me to understand as though a line had been drawn in the sand, if I believed in Him, there was to be no more crying, if I believed in Him there would be no more depression, I was going to build this army of people in prayer Tim was talking about and believe that I WAS NOT GOING TO BURY MY DAUGHTER!! That night I could not sleep. I kept thinking of my conversation with Tim and his words went through my mind over and over again. The Lord spoke to me through Tim and it had sparked something big within me. I was determined to recruit this army of prayer warriors.

The following day, I began building the army of people in prayer. I asked everyone, from visitors, to hospital employees and the like to please pray for Bella. I called Ralph Gazitua, my friend Andy's father who is a deacon at our church to come and pray with us. Ralph came with his wife, Cookie, Andy with his wife Sara. We prayed together and he also brought us some very important and encouraging words. He told us that it was important that everyone who surrounded Bella and entered her room be thinking positively. He told us that we could not allow any negative thoughts to be around us. He advised us to tell others to not cry in front of Bella and to compose themselves before they entered the room. He told us to tell people that Bella was going to walk one day and that she was not going to die and that if they did not believe that, they would not be allowed to enter. This truly touched and inspired Shannah. She made a sign and posted it on Bella's door that read in big red letters "Happy Thoughts Only!" We would take this sign back and forth from the hospital and would post it on the front door of our home as well.

Thank God, on the subsequent rounds of chemo, Bella did very well. It was a huge relief to see her accept the chemo so well, especially given what I thought was a reaction with the first dose. She never vomited and her body adjusted to the poison that was being given to her everyday. Bella did unfortunately have persistent complications with her medi-port, a titanium valve that was surgically implanted under skin in order to administer chemotherapy. It would often become "infiltrated." This meant that the needle from the IV would pop out of the port and get lodged in her chest. This would cause significant swelling in her chest and meant that treatment would be delayed as we would have to wait for the swelling to subside and then have to re-access her port with the needle. Bella absolutely hated this, as it was painful and scary. What child or adult for that matter, is fond of needles? Bella was terrified about anything that dealt with her port. Our hearts would break to see her so scared, but we knew it had to be done. Nonetheless, we all persevered.

After two weeks in the hospital beginning on the first day she became paralyzed, we finished her first full round of chemo and were to be going home. This meant that we had to make drastic changes to the way life was at home prior to the beginning of this journey. Because Bella's immune system was compromised, we had to be extremely careful with her not to get sick. This meant that we had to get rid of all of our animals. We had three small dogs and two parrots at the time. We immediately had to make arrangements to give them to friends and family to watch for the next year. Bella loved her pets and we knew she would not understand why they were being taken away from her. We too had grown close to our pets and it was not easy parting with them. However, as adults we could understand it. Because Bella was paralyzed, it meant that she would be spending a lot of time on the floor. We had a team of people come in and sanitize our floors, just to be safe. We also had hand sanitizer in every corner of our house and insisted that the few visitors we would have at home would remove their shoes outside. We had a medical supply company deliver Bella's little wheel chair and an electric hospital bed which we put right next to ours. Rayna, who was now two years old, also wanted to sleep with us and it was not fair to make her sleep in her room alone when Bella would be right there with us. Consequently, we moved Rayna's bed into our room also. This meant we had to rearrange all the furniture in the master bedroom and the room looked like one big bed. While these changes were drastic, and having Bella in a wheelchair was difficult, we were happy to be home. We live on a lake and it just so happened that the month before Bella became paralyzed, we had a dump truck bring in a large amount of sand to create a beach behind our home. All the neighborhood children would come to play behind our home. What was very difficult to watch was how Bella, who only three weeks prior could walk and play with her friends in the sand, was now immobile and in a wheelchair. It reminded me of what a beautiful bird confined to a cage must ponder, not being allowed to fly free and enjoy the spacious sky the way it did prior to it's capture. During this time she was so cute. In the evenings when the sun had gone down, we would wheel Bella outside to watch her friends. She would say hello to them and would tell them, "I slipped." She was very self conscious about her legs; she would cover them with a blanket and did not want anyone to look at them.

As soon as we got home, Shannah and I took action on those faithful words that Tim Downing spoke to me. Shannah, my sister-in- law Kim, and others, made flyers with Bella's picture asking for nothing more than prayer. Shannah and I passed these flyers out everywhere we went. We took them to the girl's school, which was the Jewish Community Center at the time, we took them to church, the supermarket and even went door to door. At first many people would not accept the flyer or would try to avoid us because they thought we were selling something. No matter what, we persevered. I still remember watching Shannah late into the evening go out into our neighborhood, knocking on doors of people she did not know passing out fliers. We were continuously building that army of people in prayer that Tim had told me about. People would constantly ask us, what can we do for you? Is there any way I can help you? We knew that the only thing we needed was a miracle. We did not need food, we did not need toys or coloring books, we didn't even need money, we needed a MIRACLE. The only thing anyone could do to help us achieve that was prayer. By the grace of God, people responded. People of all denominations, religions and ways of life agreed to pray. The great caveat we would put on our request is that we wanted them to commit to asking others to pray for us as well. Everyone agreed; it was amazing. Around this time, Ralph and Kim started a Caringbridge website for Bella. www. PrayforBella.com Now with this website people from all over the world learned of Bella and began praying for her. It was amazing to see the number of visitors that were hitting her website and posting their encouraging words of support.

A family member arranged for the Heralds of the Gospel, which is a local Catholic ministry, to bring a statue of Our Lady of Fatima, the Virgin Mary to visit our home. We had a small group of family, friends and neighbors join us to pray the Holy Rosary together. Shannah who was Jewish, learned to pray the Holy Rosary and the Heralds of the Gospel left us a very nice picture of the Virgin Mary which we put in our bedroom.

One day we received a box in the mail. Enclosed was a statuette of St. Peregrine, who was an Italian priest who lived in the 17th century and was miraculously cured of cancer. He is the Patron saint of cancer patients in the Catholic Church. Accompanying the statue was a very nice letter from a colleague at work who explained that this statue was a gift from a friend of her aunt's who was battling breast cancer. She had heard of Bella's case and felt that a child deserved to have this statue of St. Peregrine more than she. We were overwhelmed that people we didn't even know where praying for us and reaching out to us. We placed the small figurine statue in our bedroom where it still remains.

Bella continued on her 54- week treatment protocol of chemotherapy every week. Some weeks she would have to stay five nights in the hospital, some two nights, and others she would receive her chemo in the outpatient clinic. Kim would fly or drive from Orlando to Miami to stay with Bella every time she had to stay in the hospital overnight so we could go home at night to sleep with Rayna. She did this for 13 months and has been such an angel of God. Kim, who is related to us by marriage, has done more for Bella than many of those who share the same blood. Many people don't understand why and how Kim has given so much of herself to this cause. Of course, if you truly know Kim, it comes as no surprise. She is a wonderful loving person who makes every attempt to see through the eyes of God.

While Bella's treatment protocol called for radiation to begin on week 20, the oncology team at Miami Children's Hospital had a theory that if perhaps radiation was given to her spine on week 7, it may more quickly reduce the large tumor around her spinal cord and perhaps give her spinal cord the ability to heal. We were informed that Miami Children's Hospital did not offer radiation, however all cases were referred to the hospital affiliated with the University of Miami. This hospital is the county hospital for Miami and the best way I can describe it by saying is that it is very busy. The traffic in the area is congested, it is not close to our home and it has a tremendous volume of people coming in and out. Nonetheless, we went to our original radiation consultation on week 4 of Bella's protocol.

At our consultation, for which we had to wait three hours to be seen even with an appointment, the radiation oncologists informed us that their plan was to give Bella conventional radiation everyday for 5 weeks to her entire spine. She would have to be under anesthesia, intubated and ventilated everyday. She would more than likely suffer severe side effects including skin burn and disfiguration of the spine. In addition, her vocal cords would be severely damaged. I thought to myself, "How could I, as a father, allow this to be done to Bella? She had just begun to speak with all of her speech delays and now this?" As the doctors explained this to us, Shannah and I were in disbelief. I asked if they had every intubated a child everyday for so long. They said they had done it only once before. We felt as if we were stuck between a rock and a hard place. It seemed like if the cancer doesn't kill her, then the treatment protocol would. The mere thought of having to undergo this process EVERYDAY for 5 weeks straight, just seemed bizarre. As you can imagine, we left the consultation, tired, scared, frustrated and determined that there had to be another way. As we discussed our concerns with the team at Miami Children's Hospital, they explained the rationale for breaking the protocol and using the radiation early. They were determined in their logic to break the protocol and use radiation on her spine on week 7. Shannah and I eventually accepted the fact that the nightmarish treatment the University of Miami outlined could become a reality. Every way we turned, we encountered the unknown and faced the uncertain. These treatments are not guarantees they are just protocols. So, I am being asked to put my little girl through all this and there is a chance it may not solve the problem? Lord, why me?

Bella's protocol called for her first evaluation, which consisted of an MRI of spine and PET scan, since the initiation of treatment, on week 6. Shannah and I prayed that the evaluation when it was performed would show improvement so that this crazy radiation scheme as we termed it would have to be postponed, changed or not necessary at all.

Week 4 of Bella's treatment was typical of our days during that time. She was inpatient for five nights receiving chemo and by now we had become accustomed to living in and out of the hospital. Kim was always with Bella to help her in all ways possible. Bella was tolerating the chemo well and the only issue that persisted was the problems with her medi-port. On Sunday of that week, Bella was to complete her five nights of treatment and we were planning to go home in the morning. However her medi-port once again became infiltrated and because of the delay and the process I mentioned earlier, we were not discharged until about 7:30 PM. At the time of discharge, Bella's blood test showed that her hemoglobin was 8 (normal is between 10-13) and her white blood cell count (WBC) was 1.9 or 1,900 (normal is above 5,000). Bella was scheduled to have another round of chemo (week 5) on Tuesday of that coming week. Because it was less than a full 48 hours away, the doctor informed us that it was impossible that Bella's blood counts would recover in such short time. He informed us that Bella's counts would drop even further because of the chemo she had just received and that rather than have chemo on Tuesday, she would most likely require a blood transfusion. We were very disappointed because we wanted to get that last round of chemo finished, prior to the first evaluation we were so anxiously awaiting on week 6. Again, the importance of this evaluation was that we hoped that the treatment that she had received thus far would show good results and the crazy radiation scheme would not be necessary. Nonetheless, with or without the chemo and regardless of whatever the evaluation would demonstrate, Bella's medical team was ready to begin radiation on week 7.

We arrived home exhausted and immediately went to sleep. This is when the most amazing events I have ever experienced in my life began to take place, and a true miracle began to unfold right before our very eyes.

"MOMMY CHURCH"

That night, Sunday, the 12th of August 2007 at about 11:30 PM, Bella awoke in the dark and said to Shannah in a relatively loud voice and perfectly clear, "Mommy the church carries me, the church takes care of me." Shannah mumbled to Bella half asleep, "that's nice Bella, who told you that?" She said "her." At this point Shannah noticed that Bella was completely awake, and turned on the lamp by the bed. She asked her again, "Bella, who told you that?" Bella immediately pointed without hesitation to the picture of the Virgin Mary which we had in our room given to us by the Heralds of the Gospel on their earlier visit to our home. Shannah got out of bed, brought the photograph closer to Bella and said, "She told you that?" Bella answered "yes." At this point Bella asked in a tone and vocabulary not of her own, to please give her these two small statuettes that were on our dresser. One of the statues was a small porcelain figurine of the Virgin Mary which someone gave us while we were in the hospital in the very early days of Bella's diagnosis; the other was the statue of St. Peregrine. Bella began to role play with these figurines. She took Mary and placed her face over Peregrine's leg and made a kissing sound with her lips. She then turned to Shannah and said in the clearest voice we have ever heard Bella speak in, "Mommy, booboos are all gone." She then returned the figurines to Shannah and immediately went to sleep, Shannah turned off the light and we laid there in shock. A short while later, Bella awoke again and turned to her and again in a vocabulary and tone not of her said "Mommy the booboos are not all gone yet, but they will be very soon." Then, Bella whose legs were absolutely paralyzed spontaneously kicked Shannah and proclaimed "Mommy I did it!" She then again fell asleep. Shannah and I laid there in disbelief of what we were witnessing. Shannah alone and in the dark began to pray the Holy Rosary silently. Bella awoke a third time, aggressively snatched the Holy Rosary from Shannah's hand and said "Mommy that's hers."

I don't know how Shannah and I slept afterward. We were in shock and not quite sure of what had just transpired in our bed room. Was all of this a dream? Could Bella have somehow been dreaming and speaking in her sleep? Yet the tone of her voice was unlike that we had ever heard before. Her vocabulary seemed so advanced for Bella. In the morning, Bella began talking at length about someone named "Mommy Church." She said that Mommy Church was wearing red and had a baby. She said that Mommy Church was going to help her walk again and that she carried her. Shannah and I continued to speak to the many family members and friends who called us on a daily basis to check up on us, but we did not tell anyone of what was happening with Bella because we did not want anyone to think we had lost our minds. I can assure you that no one taught Bella about the Virgin Mary or anything she had spoken of. Shannah was Jewish. Bella and Rayna both had been attending the Jewish community center, so they did not teach that there and I had been away from practicing my faith for quite some time. We did not have pictures of Mary or Jesus in our house. We did not even have as much as a cross or crucifix up until this point. In addition, Bella was speaking clearly, in complete sentences and different tone and vocabulary than ever before. This is a child that was in speech therapy and could not speak in full sentences. How was it possible that she spoke to us the way she did? It was all such a mystery, but it would eventually be revealed.

Because I am Catholic, I explained to Shannah after Bella repeatedly mentioned "Mommy Church" that Catholics believe that the Virgin Mary is the mother of Jesus and the Catholic Church and has appeared on earth in different places over the history of time in different vestibules. I suggested that we show Bella some pictures of the different appearances of Mary and see how she reacted. I printed from the internet, a picture of Our Lady of Lourdes, Our Lady of Charity, Our Lady of Fatima and Our Lady of Guadalupe. Bella kept insisting that Mommy Church had a baby. As soon as we showed Bella the image of Our Lady of Guadalupe, she immediately identified the baby as the angel at the bottom of the image under Our Lady's feet. She clearly identified Our Lady of Guadalupe as "Mommy Church." In our amazement, I researched further information about Our Lady of Guadalupe on the internet. I learned that the feast day of Our Lady of Guadalupe is December 12th. We could not believe it. Bella was born on December 12th!

We learned that in the year 1531 a "Lady from Heaven" appeared to a humble Native American at Tepeyac, a hill northwest of what is now Mexico City. She identified herself as the ever virgin Holy Mary, Mother of the True God for whom we live, the Creator of all things, Lord of heaven and the earth. She made a request for a church to be built on the site, and submitted her wish by way of the Indian Juan Diego to the local Bishop. When the Bishop hesitated, and requested from her a sign, the Mother of God obeyed without delay or question and sent her native messenger to the top of the hill in mid-December to gather an assortment of roses for the Bishop. After complying to the Bishop's request for a sign, she also left for us an image of herself imprinted miraculously on the native's *tilma*, a poor quality cactus-cloth garment, which should have deteriorated in 20 years but shows no sign of decay 476 years later and still defies all scientific explanations of its origin.

An incredible list of miracles, cures and interventions are attributed to her intercession. Yearly, between 18 - 20 million pilgrims visit the Basilica of Guadalupe in Mexico City, making it Christianity's most visited sanctuary.

Bella continued to refer to Mary as "Mommy Church" and repeated frequently that "Mommy Church" was going to help her walk again soon. The following night, Monday the 13th of August

A black and white copy of the original image of Our Lady of Guadalupe
which was miraculously imprinted on the tilma of Juan Diego in 1531

2007 at approximately 11 PM, while asleep, Bella woke up and screamed "No, I want to sleep with Mary!" and fell immediately back to sleep. On Tuesday the 14th of August 2007, we took Bella to her scheduled appointment at the oncology clinic. When we walked into the office, the nurse greeted us and referred to Bella's discharge notes that were in her chart. She said to us as she read the chart "Oh yeah, you guys are scheduled for chemo, but will have a blood transfusion instead." I responded, "She hasn't had a Cell Blood Count (CBC) yet, I guess we will know what will happen after that. She agreed, and Bella proceeded to phlebotomy, where she had her blood extracted for the CBC. As we waited in the examination room for the doctor, my aunt, Josefina, who is affectionately known to all as "Fifi", who works in the laboratory of the hospital, brought us the results before the doctor had received them. To everyone's amazement, her hemoglobin had risen to 10 (9.9) and her white blood count had risen to 12, 700 (12.7). Dr. Escalon walked in shortly thereafter surprised to see these high counts. He was in disbelief. Nonetheless, Bella did not need a transfusion and she qualified to have her chemo, which she did! That afternoon, I spoke with my father who had already been communicated the lab results by my aunt. He also was in disbelief of how her hemoglobin and white blood cell count rose in such a short period of time and right after chemo. It was then that I felt comfortable telling him of the incredible events that had occurred at our house with Bella and "Mommy Church." He was surprised, but by faith believed what I was saying.

That afternoon, Bella told her 19-year-old cousin, Christian, "Mommy Church will help me walk soon." She also said "I saw the angel walk through the wall." Christian asked where this happened. Bella answered "at the hospital." Christian asked if the angel had wings, Bella answered "no." During the night while asleep, Bella awoke and screamed, "Thank you, Jesus, help me walk again!" On Wednesday, the 15th of August 2007, in the parking garage of Miami Children's Hospital at approximately 10:30 AM, Bella again, seemed odd. She became very serious, looked in my eyes and told me "Mommy Church is going to help me walk very soon." I noticed that whenever Bella was going to say something profound with regards to her improvement she would typically stop whatever she was doing. She would suddenly get quiet and serious, then speak.

That evening, August 15th 2007, Shannah and I attended Mass at St. John Neumann where I went to school and attended church periodically. During those days, we would pray with anyone and would attend church services anywhere. We heard that there was to be a Mass that evening at our church and planned to go. We found it odd that there was Mass on Wednesday evening, but we did not ask questions and attended. We immediately realized as the service began that this was Feast of the Assumption of Mary. During the homily given by Monsignor Pablo Navarro, Shannah says she had a vision of the Blessed Mother carrying Bella and presenting her to Christ. Shannah said that Jesus looked at her and said "I will save her, but you must serve me." As soon as the Mass ended Shannah told me of her vision and that she wanted to convert to Catholicism. I knew at this point that I had to tell someone in the church of what we were experiencing. After the Mass, we approached Monsignor Navarro. We were afraid. I knew who he was, but I knew that he had no idea who we were; we had no relationship with the church. Ignorant to the amount of people who like to greet Monsignor Navarro after every Mass, we cut the line and interrupted. I said to myself, "I have to tell this man what has been happening, he might think I'm crazy but I have to tell somebody from the church what was happening at our house with Bella." We introduced ourselves and told him we were Bella's parents. Before we could give more details about Bella, he told us that he knew of Bella and that the church office had received a flyer with Bella's picture on it and were praying for her. I briefly explained what had been happening at our home with Bella and "Mommy Church." Monsignor Navarro looked deeply into my eyes and said "would you be open to me visiting your home some day?" I said, "Absolutely." He asked me to write down my cell phone number and address on a piece of paper. We left and I wasn't sure if the Monsignor believed me or not. At 9:00 PM to our pleasant surprise, Monsignor Navarro called me and asked me, would now be appropriate for a visit? I said "yes!" I was simply amazed that he responded so quickly. I would later learn how busy a man he is and what an honor it was for us to have him visit us so spontaneously.

It was a pleasure to have Monsignor in our home. We showed Monsignor where everything had been happening in the house and he gathered us in prayer around Bella, he laid hands on her and it was a very special visit. He called us every week to check in on Bella from that day forward.

The following night, while asleep, Bella awoke and screamed "I love you Jesus, thank you!" she again fell immediately to sleep. The following day, Friday the 17th of August 2007, Bella told her 19-year-old cousin Christian, again in a voice not typical of her, "Mommy church is my mommy, and she helps me." Before going to bed that Friday at 9:35 PM, Bella spoke to us very clearly and said, "When they take the pictures, the booboos will be all gone." While we did not fully understand what was happening to Bella, we could feel the presence of God every time Bella had an episode. Our faith was increasing that Bella was going to be healed and that God had and has a very special plan for her. We did tell some close family members of what was happening but were still reluctant to tell many others because, as I mentioned earlier, unfortunately when you live what we were living at that time, many lose their mind.

When Bella was diagnosed with cancer we received as a gift a relic of blessed Fr. Xavier Frances Seelos from a woman who was a 3 time cancer survivor and friends with Ralph and Kim. We frequently would place this relic on Bella's spine above the scar from her spinal surgery. At approximately 3:00 AM on Sunday the 19th of August, Bella began to radiate a tremendous amount of heat. Because she was sleeping in between Shannah and I, the high temperature we were feeling awakened us both. We were warned by all her doctors that if Bella developed a fever at anytime, that we were to go to the Emergency Room at once. Afraid that Bella had developed fever, we took her temperature. Unbelievably, her temperature was normal. We realized that the epicenter of the heat was where the relic remained on her back. We stayed up for several hours to take Bella's temperature. Every time we measured, it was normal at 98 degrees. How could so much heat be generated from a small body and yet no fever seems to register on the thermometer? It didn't seem possible, but it would be confirmed that with God all things are possible!

On Monday the 20th of August, we were looking forward to having Bella's MRI of the spine the following day per week 6 of the protocol. I had this feeling that I again wanted to unite people in prayer especially the night before the scan. I initially had the idea of gathering as many people as possible at our home to pray. Later, an idea, no doubt inspired by the Holy Spirit, entered my mind. In my field of work, conference calls with hundreds of people were common. I thought "we can't just have a small group praying at our house about the scan tomorrow, people from everywhere are praying for her." I had the idea of organizing a conference call so that way hundreds of people could pray together at the same time. I told Shannah and Ralph and Kim of the idea and they contacted Fr. Gregory Parkes who is a dear friend of Ralph and Kim's and is the pastor of Corpus Christi parish and the Chancellor of the Orlando diocese. Fr. Gregory agreed to lead the call and Shannah and I began to spread the word that we would have a prayer teleconference for Bella's scan the following day. That evening we had over 150 callers and more than 200 people praying in unison as Fr. Gregory led the call reading scripture, leading everyone in prayer as a community of faith. Prior to this call, and after I came to faith because of my friend Tim Downing, I hadn't cried. However, hearing so many people logging on to attend this call for my daughter and my family, overwhelmed me with emotion and humility. As the call proceeded, I was on my knees, with tears in my eyes in our living room. There were people from everywhere in the United States on the call and even some from Puerto Rico and South America. It was incredible to see so many people come together in faith to pray for Bella and our family. There were also many people of different faiths and almost every Christian denomination. Believers and non-believers were all on the same phone lines listening to sacred scripture and asking

God to cure Bella. Everyone was praying in unison and storming the heavens with prayer.

Prior to the call that afternoon, I spoke to a member of the team at Miami Children's Hospital. She is a renowned physician and a great friend of our family. I told her how excited I was about Bella's first evaluation since starting treatment. To my disappointment, she told me that she did not think that we should do the test. She told me that it had only been 5 weeks of treatment and that Bella would have to been put under anesthesia for the test. She said that it was too soon and that we should probably wait to have a scan. I told her that I was positive about what the test would show. I told her that I wanted to see that the treatment Bella had done so far had been so effective that the "crazy radiation scheme" that was scheduled for the following week would be postponed. I was hopeful that we would see great results. She looked at me with sadness in her eyes and said "Raymond, I am glad that you are so optimistic; you know that I love you. Understand that this is a stage 4 Rhabdomyosarcoma. This has spread throughout Bella's body and has been growing and living very comfortably. If we see that the cancer hasn't spread over the past 5 weeks, you can consider that a victory." She also told me "remember Raymond, this is no ones fault, if this does not work out and she dies, it is not your fault." I told her that I insisted on the scan and she agreed with my wishes. I did leave a little deflated from the meeting. Given how well Bella was withstanding the treatment so far with virtually no side effects other than hair loss, it was hard for me to hear how the doctors fully believed that little if anything could stop the cancer growing inside her. I realize that doctors must give you the facts but what I had been observing in my daughter had made me optimistic.

On Tuesday the 21st of August, Bella had an MRI of her spine to determine the effects of the treatment on the tumor around her spine. It was a very tense day as you can imagine for our entire family, particularly for Shannah and I. As we awaited the results in a room on the oncology floor about thirty minutes after the scan; I will never forget my father, walking in with tears in his eyes shouting "The tumor has shrunk about 90%, this is incredible!" We hugged each other praising God and thanking "Mommy Church for her prayers." None of her doctors could explain this wonderful result. I remember, receiving a call from my boss, Sheri Jepsen right at that moment; I told her the news. I was crying tears of joy as was she. It was an incredible moment. 90% in such a short time seemed amazing! We were totally uplifted and it strengthened our faith even further to see such progress being made. We left the hospital later that afternoon and went home to rest and spend the night. We were so happy to share the wonderful news on Bella's website and with all our family, friends and Bella's prayer warriors.

On Thursday, the 23rd of August 2007, Bella was to have a PET scan to determine the effects of treatment on all of her metastasis (shoulder, jaw, rib, hip, knee, foot and hand) my father and I were with Bella when she was put under anesthesia for the test around 7:00 AM. Once she was in the machine for the scan, we went to the doctor's lounge to have breakfast. There I saw Dr. Escalon, the Chief of Oncology. He said to me, "Raymond, the results from Tuesday's MRI are incredible, however I want you to know that all of Bella's metastasis have been on the bones. These type of metastasis respond even more slowly to chemo, so we don't expect to see any changes at all today, given it has been so soon since she started treatment." I told him that I understood and my father and I finished breakfast. We proceeded to the lobby of the hospital and Shannah, who had slept at home with Rayna, joined us shortly thereafter.

While we waited, both Shannah and I prayed the Holy Rosary separately. My father also was praying on his own. While I prayed the Holy Rosary, something extraordinary happened. I felt something I have never felt in my life prior and have never felt since. I felt an uncomfortable pressure on my neck and shoulders and I started to hear a voice. The voice became louder and louder, "They will look and not find it, they will look and not find it." I have felt God guide me before in my life to do certain things and avoid certain things, but this was different. I was actually <u>hearing</u> a voice! It was as real and present to me at that time, as it is for you as you read these lines. I knew that I was not going crazy because of the things that had been ongoing at our house with Bella, and

I answered, "Our Lady of Guadalupe, if this is so, I will go to Mexico City were your Basilica is and praise your Son and thank you in person next week."

Two hours later, my father who had been given the results by the radiologists, came with a tremendous smile on his face and said to us in a loud voice "It's all gone, the cancer is gone! Every site except the significantly reduced tumor on the spine, is all gone, It's not visible on the scan, they cannot find it!" The impossible had become reality. All of her metastasis where not visible on the scan and after further study of the MRI that had been done on Tuesday, the main tumor on her spine had actually been reduced 94%. This meant that Bella was responding incredibly well to treatment, this meant that our prayers were being answered and we were all witnessing a miracle. This also meant that the "crazy radiation scheme" had been canceled and we would continue on the chemo protocol. PRAISE GOD! THANK YOU JESUS!

As we were leaving the hospital; employees from different departments were congratulating us. Some people were screaming "Alleluia" in the hallways! It was an incredible feeling. We felt that there was light at the end of the dark tunnel. We drove straight to St. John Neumann Catholic Church which was now our home parish. We drove with the windows down, praising God and screaming for joy! We were looking to share the good and amazing news with all and particularly, Monsignor Navarro. When we arrived, we prayed with two of the parish priests, Fr. Kiddy and Fr. Carmelo and the church office staff. Monsignor Navarro was at his home which is very close to the church. We hated to visit him unannounced, but we had to see him. When we arrived he welcomed us and was so happy. I will never forget what he said to me. I said "Monsignor, it's a miracle! They cannot find the cancer!" He said to me ever so calming and reassuring, "Raymond, this is what we have been praying for, a miracle, why are you so surprised?" What an amazing example of faith Monsignor Navarro has been for me and our family.

That evening once the girls had gone to sleep, I recounted to Shannah what had happened to me while I was in prayer at the hospital. I told her of the voice that I heard and the promise I made. I told her that I had to book my flight to go to Mexico to visit the Basilica of our Lady of Guadalupe next week. Shannah understood and while the last thing she wanted was for me to travel out of the country at that time, she was supportive. Bella had the following few days off from treatment and we were going to continue physical therapy and occupational therapy at home which we had arranged and were ongoing between visits and stays at the hospital. I booked my flight for the following Wednesday. I planned to leave on an early flight to Mexico City and return to Miami on a 5:00 PM flight that same day.

On Sunday the 26th of August at approximately 7:00 PM, Bella and I were lying in bed playing. Bella again spoke in a vocabulary and tone not her own. This followed the same pattern as the other times. She, who was giggling and laughing with me in bed, suddenly looked deep into my eyes, became very serious and spoke very clearly, "Very soon Daddy." I asked her, "Very soon what Bella?" She answered "Mommy Church will help me walk very soon." I said, "I know Bella, when you see Mommy Church, tell her we love her very much." To my surprise, Bella fell asleep shortly thereafter. I did not expect her to fall asleep so early and expected her to stay up a little longer. When she fell asleep all the lights in the bedroom where room on. About 25 minutes later, as she was sleeping and I was lying next to her and praying over her quietly, she suddenly awoke and screamed "I love you Jesus!" She immediately fell back to sleep. My emotions were high and my adrenalin was also. Imagine being there with your child sleeping only to awake abruptly and hear her scream such beautiful words. Because she remained asleep, I exited quietly to tell Shannah what had just happened. As I was explaining to Shannah what had just occurred, Rayna who was playing in the kitchen and making noise started walking towards the bedroom. Shannah and I ran after Rayna so that she would not enter the room and wake Bella. Rayna made it into the room making noise as we caught up to her. Bella woke up as we entered the room and said "Fatima, Jesus? Fatima, Jesus? Fatima, Jesus?" As she said this, she had her eyes open and was looking around the room as though they had suddenly disappeared and had just been in her sight. This was very astounding as we had not discussed anything of Fatima (Our Lady of Fatima) in the house since the Heralds of the Gospel brought the image of Fatima to our home shortly following Bella's diagnosis. We had certainly discussed Guadalupe in front of her, but not Fatima. Nonetheless, it was an amazing occurrence and Shannah and I praised God for being with Bella and sending his Mother to comfort her and be with her.

On Wednesday the 29th of August 2007 I departed for Mexico City from Miami on an early morning flight, scheduled tor return to Miami at 5:00 PM. As I sat on the plane, I prayed fervently in thanksgiving for the wonderful results of Bella's MRI and PET scan. I prayed the Holy Rosary and felt incredible inner peace. This flight experience was new for me. I was not going to a business meeting, for which I usually review business material while in the air. I was not going on a vacation; I was going to fulfill a promise and give thanks to God and honor "Mommy Church."

Prior to this, in mid July, my father and Ralph went to Mexico City on a business trip. They were only going for 3 days, but one of the main objectives my brother had was to visit the shrine and make a petition for my daughter Bella. Between business appointments, they managed to make it to the Basilica of Our Lady of Guadalupe. Ralph had been to Mexico City on a few occasions, but had only visited the basilica on one occasion. It was during his honeymoon and he had made the mistake of wearing shorts. The basilica maintains a very strict dress code and those who are not dressed appropriately are not allowed to enter. Well, 20 years had passed since Ralph had been there. Upon arrival, the Mass was being celebrated and Ralph describes a feeling of overwhelming emotion as he entered the sanctuary. Tears ran down his face as he laid eyes on the *tilma* of Saint Juan Diego, which is where the image of the Blessed Mother, Our Lady of Guadalupe, appeared almost 500 years ago. The cloth is preserved and hung behind the high altar for everyone to see. It is truly an amazing sight and thousands of people pray before the image.

Their time at the basilica was very limited, so they quickly bought some candles that would be lit for numerous petitions that Ralph bought with him to Mexico. After lighting the candles at the grottos, they both headed to the old Basilica, which is located next door to the modern basilica where the *tilma* is kept. As they entered the old basilica, Ralph noticed that off to the side of the main sanctuary, the Blessed Sacrament was exposed and a few faithful adored the consecrated body of Christ. Ralph asked my father to wait for him and he went in and knelt before the Blessed Sacrament. There he prayed with great intensity asking Jesus to cure Bella and have her walk again. He also prayed for his son, Christian, who had encountered some problems that there was great concern over. After a few minutes, Ralph joined my father, and the two went before a large, framed print of Our Lady of Guadalupe. There at her feet, were many, many photographs of children and adults left there by loved ones. There were small candles that had been lit and the candlelight radiated against the many photographs. Ralph felt this was the perfect place to put Bella and Christian's photograph. My father and brother knelt at a small wooden kneeler and made their petitions known to God. They asked the Blessed Mother to please intercede and bring these petitions to her son, Jesus. It was emotional, it was solemn, and it felt like a mission completed. They needed to leave for their afternoon of meetings, but not before Ralph managed to visit one of the many souvenir and religious articles store and load up on rosaries, prints, key chains, and other trinkets. The taxi driver was an older gentleman who had patiently walked and waited with them all the while they were at the shrine. He too said some prayers and graciously provided a little bit of history as they walked through the enormous plaza towards the taxi. My father vowed on that day that, if Bella were able to walk again, someday we would all return as a family to the shrine and have Bella place flowers at Our Lady's feet.

I landed in Mexico City at approximately 10:30AM. As I quickly passed customs and immigration, I was amazed to see how updated the airport was. I had not been in Mexico for approximately 12 years, the technological improvements and booming economic development was stunning. I remembered that in my previous travels to Mexico, I was always warned to pick a reputable taxi service as in the past tourists were hijacked and robbed by taxi drivers. As I exited the airport there was now concierge guides from the Mexican Department of Transportation that put me in a licensed taxi. As soon as I entered the taxi and smiled at the driver, I knew I was safe.

The driver asked me were I was traveling and I answered "La Basilica de Guadalupe, por favor." I am fully bilingual so communicating in Spanish is not a problem. He began driving and then asked "how many days will you be in Mexico?" I told him that I had a return flight to Miami at 5:00 PM. He asked me if I was in Mexico for business. I told him that I came to Mexico because I was fulfilling a promise. I told him that my 4-year-old daughter had cancer and was paralyzed and that I had made a promise to the Virgin Mary to come visit her last week. He was a little taken aback by my response and said to me, "Sir it's nearly 11:00 AM, the basilica is not too far away but there is a lot of traffic. You must be back at the airport at least 2 hours before an international flight; you don't have a lot of time." I said I understood, and if necessary I would sleep in Mexico that night, but I had to get to the basilica as soon as possible.

The driver increased his speed and focused on getting there. He navigated the very congested traffic of Mexico City. He continued reassuring me that although the traffic was bad, we were not very far and that we should be arriving soon. I began to tell him that my daughter had been speaking of Our Lady of Guadalupe. I explained to him that my daughter had seven metastasis throughout her body and now none was visible on her scan. I told him that she was paralyzed but that Bella was saying that "Mommy Church" was going to help her walk soon. When I told him that Bella was born on December 12th, he almost drove off the road! He told me that it didn't surprise him that much though. He had other passengers over the years tell him about miracles that have occurred and that he and his family, as is typical of many Mexicans, were very devoted to Guadalupe.

As we approached the basilica, he continued to reassure me that we were almost there. He explained to me that typically we would be seeing the roof of the main sanctuary but that the trees had grown in such a way that it was now blocking the view, but not to worry, we were almost there. The anticipation of finally going before the image of our Lady on the *tilma*, made my heart race. I felt so happy that I was about to fulfill the promise that I had made.

When I left for Mexico, I contemplated not bringing my cell phone. I didn't think I would have cell service, therefore I didn't think I would need it. Nonetheless out of habit and because I figured, in case of an emergency, if there was service, it might come in handy, so I took it with me. At the very moment that I arrived at the basilica and I saw the building, while I was still in the taxi my Blackberry® rang. It was Shannah, she was screaming with joy! She informed me that at that very instant, Bella who was completely paralyzed from the waist down when I left Miami only a few hours prior, had gotten up and began crawling all around the house!

I was again overcome with emotion and joy and praised God. I stood at the entrance to the Massive courtyard, which leads to the main sanctuary. To my right there was a large group of women who had come on a pilgrimage to the Basilica assembled in a corner of the courtyard, singing *Ave Maria*, it was beautiful. As I beheld what was before me, filled with emotion, I also saw some women crossing the courtyard heading toward the main church on their knees, carrying newborn infants. I had seen this phenomenon in videos on the Internet about the basilica. It is amazing how devoted the Mexican women, are to Guadalupe, that they cross the courtyard, crawl up the steps and enter the church not only on their bare knees on the hard, uneven concrete, but also carrying their newborn children to dedicate them to Christ and ask for the protection of Our Lady of Guadalupe. Many of these women are bleeding at the knees, as the rough stone in the courtyard takes its toll on their flesh. As I stood there observing this incredible demonstration of faith, I could feel the presence of God. This moment is the defining moment of my life. At that very moment, I knew that what we had been experiencing was a true miracle, I knew God had heard our prayers and that I had kept my promise, I knew that God had healed my daughter and I knew that BELLA WOULD WALK AGAIN! Between the news I had just received about Bella crawling, the women singing beautifully and the women on their knees in the courtyard, I felt as though I was living a dream. I immediately came to the realization that if there was anyone who should be on his knees there, it was me. I dropped to my knees with my back pack on and walked on my knees with those women into the church. As I approached I could see large letters on the entrance, which said, "Am I not here who am your mother?" These are the words that Guadalupe spoke to Juan Diego in 1531.

As I entered the very large and breathtakingly beautiful church, I could see the *tilma* with Our Lady's image in the distance behind the altar. I crawled on my knees to the last row of pews that comprised the main seating area in the church. I prayed very fervently there and thanked God for his mercy upon me and my family. I also thanked and honored Mary for comforting Bella, for visiting her and for interceding for her to her Son for Bella's healing. I stayed there on my knees for several minutes. I wanted to go see the *tilma* up close, but I did not feel I was ready yet. I had this excited and emotional feeling, the kind of feeling I felt on Christmas mornings when I was a kid. I walked around the main sanctuary and found one of the many chapels inside the main basilica. I entered and sat surrounded by others in front of the largest tabernacle I could ever imagine.

This is where I spent most of my time while in the basilica; in front of where the body of Christ is housed. I felt very comfortable and prayed there for a long time. I prayed in thanksgiving, I prayed for every person I have ever known and I prayed the Holy Rosary in silence. I felt incredible peace there. Once I felt ready, I finished praying, exited and walked toward the tilma.

The *tilma* is behind the main altar but it is separated by a corridor which has three conveyor belts on it that slowly move in alternating opposite motion. This exists so as to maintain a flow of the many tourists and faithful that visits the Basilica on a daily basis. There were only a handful of people there. Some were in prayer and some were taking pictures. I again dropped to my knees on the conveyor belt. I spent time there going from conveyor belt to conveyor belt and repeated dropping to my knees as I slowly passed the image of Our Lady. My prayers were of thanks, honor and love. I thanked her for visiting Bella, for keeping her under her blessed mantel and in the gaze of Christ who had healed her and raised her from paralysis.

After some time, I exited the main building and began the walk up the hill to the top of Tepeyac, which is the summit of where the basilica is located and the site of the first apparition of Our Lady of Guadalupe. This is where the original church was built and the location where the actual miracle took place in 1531. If you have never visited the Basilica, I would recommend a visit at least once in your life. Regardless of your religion or denomination it would be worthy of a trip. This is a place were the presence of God is felt and the actions of the faithful there would inspire anyone. As I began climbing the long series of stairs up the hill, I admired the stunning gardens which were once barren desert rock until after the miracle in 1531. It is a beautiful array of flowers, roses and other beautiful scenery. When I arrived at the summit, I read a sign in Spanish which reads "this is the location where the miracle took place in 1531, the ground you are walking on pilgrim is sacred, as Mary, the mother of Christ also took steps here."

I entered the quaint and beautiful church and prayed there again in thanksgiving and praise. As my time was short, I began to descend down the other side of the hill, which leads to an area where refreshments and religious souvenirs are sold. There I shopped for my family, bought some rosaries and other items. As I did this I told one of the vendors why I was there, that my daughter who was born on the 12th of December was being healed of cancer and had been lifted from paralysis. The woman embraced me and gave me a special child's scapula, which is a type of sacred necklace, as a gift for Bella. What a joyous feeling! As I continued descending the hill, I continued to observe the magnificent view of the city below and the beautiful gardens and sculptures that make up the grounds of the basilica. I once again entered the main basilica and went before the *tilma* to pray one last time before I had to leave.

Before exiting the taxi upon my arrival, I had arranged for the driver to meet me at a certain time at the same spot he dropped me. When I arrived there I did not see him, but stayed there. A man approached me and asked me "Are you going to the airport friend?" I answered, "no thank you, I am waiting for someone to pick me up." He said to me, "Are you the man with the little girl with cancer?" I was stunned, I said "yes" He said "My son picked you up at the airport, he called me after he dropped you off. He told me about your daughter, I also work with him in the taxi business and I asked him if I could take you back to the airport as I wanted to meet you and hear about your daughter." My first driver must have given him a great description of what I looked like, because the area around the basilica is busy with hoards of people. He drove me back to the airport and we had a very nice conversation about what had been ongoing with Bella. He told me that he believed in God and that he and his family attended Mass on Sundays at the Basilica. He assured me that his entire family would be praying for Bella. I arrived at the airport and returned on the plane to Miami, exhausted from my joyous emotions and the long day.

The following day, Bella was crawling all around the house. It was fantastic to see her happiness. She wanted to crawl, hated her wheelchair and was happy that now she was mobile. I felt in my heart that Bella was going to be walking again soon. Besides, she continued to tell us "Mommy Church is going to help me walk soon." She always followed a similar pattern when she said this. She would get very serious, look at us directly in the eyes and begin speaking in a clear voice and tone. This was very distinct as Bella always had a severe speech delay.

I wanted to accelerate her ability to get on her feet again as Bella's legs became stronger. I had the idea of getting Bella a walker, like an infant walker to help her learn to walk again quickly. She was receiving physical therapy at home, but the therapist couldn't bring with her the large array of equipment available at the physical therapy gym at Miami Children's Hospital. The problem was that because Bella's blood counts were so low due to the chemotherapy, the oncologist advised us not to take Bella to the hospital for physical therapy because the chances of catching a communal infection were high. Shannah and I went to stores that sold infant walkers. We bought two of them but Bella weighed 60 lbs and was very overweight at the time. Thank God she was because she lost close to 20 lbs because of her treatment and never needed an intravenous feeding tube. Indeed the Lord knows what He does. Nonetheless, the idea of the walker was going no where fast because they would not support Bella's weight. I had spoken to Ralph on the phone about a walker for Bella and shared with him my frustration in not being able to find anything for Bella. I told him I needed something that could hold her and would be higher off the ground. He said, "It almost sounds like you need a high chair without the chair."

In an effort to come up with something, I entered our very messy and disorganized garage at home. I noticed an old high chair that both girls used while they were infants. I had an idea that I could perhaps modify it. I knew that it could hold her weight and it was adjustable. I pulled the high chair out, began thinking and then prayed. I asked St. Joseph, who was Jesus' dad on earth and who was a carpenter to intercede for me and inspire me to build something to help my little girl walk again. I can assure you that my prayer was answered, as I am not a very handy guy and carpentry has to be one of my very worst skills. Nonetheless, I cut the seat off and used the legs and structure of the high chair. I attached wheels to the bottom four legs. I screwed in two wooden 2x4s in front and in back of the structure and then drilled in a strong piece of fabric so that Bella could straddle the fabric, stand and use her legs to roll and rest on the fabric if she got tired. This makeshift walker looked like something out of a wood shop class gone bad, but I thought it might work. When I emerged into the house with my invention, Shannah looked at me and said "What is that thing?" Bella, wanted to try it. I put Bella on it and while it needed to be adjusted for height and could use better casters; it worked. Bella's face lit up, she was now upright and could kick her little legs to propel herself.

We had to go to the hospital that day as Bella was going in for another 5 nights of chemo. I took my contraption walker with us. When we arrived there, the nurses looked at me and seemed to be asking themselves what junkyard I had gotten this thing from. The slick floor of the hospital proved to be ideal for the walker to roll on. I knew that it needed adjustment, so I called the physical therapist at the hospital and asked her to come up to the oncology floor. She observed from a distance Bella's gait on the walker and told me that I needed to raise the fabric. She thought my idea might just work. In our haste and my forgetfulness while leaving for the hospital, I neglected to bring my drill. This invention did not even have all the same type of screws; I had put it together with whatever screws I could find in my garage. I asked if anyone had a drill at the hospital. The answer was obvious, no. I then noticed that there was a portion of the hospital that was being remodeled. I figured it was worth a try. I walked into the secure construction zone as if I owned the place. I saw a man with a cordless drill and said "Hi, I'm with the hospital, could you be so kind as to lend me your drill and a few bit adaptors, I will return it right away." The man looked at me strangely, but said, "You're with the hospital?" "Sure", I said. I made the adjustments just as the physical therapist suggested. Bella began flying around the floor in her new walker. I felt like the best dad in the world, while my invention looked horrific and borderline dangerous, it worked beautifully. The same nurses that thought I was nuts at first were applauding my invention. Bella's happiness said it all, she could now zip back and forth on her own, and she was upright. In fact, she didn't want to get out of it. She would roll across the halls as she was getting chemo, and we had to chase her with her IV pole so that the needle wouldn't come out of her port or so that the hose wouldn't snap. She would chase the nurses and try to run over their feet with the walker, she thought it was so funny and of course they all played along with her. Bella would go and visit other children in their rooms and she was a breath of fresh air and laughter. She became an inspiration to many other parents who knew Bella had been paralyzed. Her sheer joy lifted other children and parents and gave them hope. Because she was now upright, the nurses made Bella an honorary nurse and gave her a drawer where she could keep scrap paper to draw on. She would stand behind the counter just like the nurses and even helped them file charts on occasion. Thankfully, Bella continued her chemotherapy treatments incredibly well. She was on seven different types of chemo and never vomited nor got sick and never again had a problem with her port infiltrating. We finished the five night treatment and returned home. During this time, Bella continued to improve in her walking with her walker. She wanted to be in it the entire time whether at home or at the hospital. I had to put larger wheels on it as she wanted to go outside on the side walk. While she was not allowed to get sun because of interaction with her chemotherapy, we would go outside with her at sundown so that she could enjoy some fresh air.

After a few weeks of using the walker that I made, one day I promised her a new fish for her fish tank. It was the only pet she could have since she was on chemotherapy. She and I went the fish store, as she and I call it. Next to the store was a medical supply store and I noticed a pediatric walker in the window. These walkers are the type you typically see older people pushing for balance. I had never seen one so small and honestly was so content with how she was doing in the walker I had made that I did not bother to look for other options. Nonetheless, I said "Hey Bella, come with me." I put her in the stroller I had with me and entered the store with her. I spoke to the man inside, who was the owner, and asked him if Bella could try it out in the store. While Bella was very shaky, she was able to take a few steps completely upright and she was so happy. I rented the walker and went home. We surprised Shannah, Rayna, and my parents as they only expected us to come home with a fish, and certainly not a pediatric walker. Yet we were overjoyed that she could use the walker. She had much difficulty, but was determined. You can see video of her walking in this pediatric walker on her website: www.PrayforBella.com. She was dancing and so happy to be walking around. At one point in the video she screams "AMEN, THANK YOU FOR PRAYING FOR ME!" Also interesting is that before she says "AMEN" in this video she looks over her shoulder as she is having difficulty and pain walking as though to be looking for someone. She then straightens her leg and screams AMEN! It was a wonderful day and as far as we were concerned Bella had been lifted from paralysis. If she did not improve more than this we were grateful.

Because of Bella's mental handicap, Bella suffers from what is known as a self regulation disorder. To give you an illustration of what this is like, I will give you the following example. If our family was to be in the car driving and Rayna would ask us for milk, we would simply explain that we did not have milk in the car and she would have to wait until we got home. Rayna and most children can regulate and sooth themselves, even if they have a fit at first, to wait until getting milk is possible. Bella on the other hand did not have this ability. She would scream, kick, and repeat "I want milk" over and over again. She could and would have a fit for hours unless we found some milk somewhere. She would get so upset that she at times would even pull the hair from her head. You can imagine how difficult this is to deal with especially if you are in public or over someone else's house.

During one of the manifestations of this, including pulling her hair out, which was now very brittle because of the chemo, in our master bedroom with both Shannah and I trying to console her, Bella did something she had never done before. Bella suddenly stopped crying and having a fit. She sniffed the air and said clearly in a tone not of her "I smell roses." Shannah and I were immediately in shock. Bella has never been able to identify different types of flowers and has never said the word "rose". She did this at approximately 9:30 AM and later at approximately 7:30 PM in the same location in the bed of the master bedroom. Shannah and I never smelled the roses, however both episodes followed the same pattern of her changing her voice, sniffing the air and speaking clearly saying "I smell roses."

The following week while Bella was inpatient undergoing chemo, one of her nurses walked into the room with a rose in her pocket. I do not know who gave her the rose, however Shannah asked to borrow it for a moment. Shannah took the rose to Bella who was in the hospital bed and asked her, "Bella what is this?" Bella answered in her usual tone and limited vocabulary "a flowler." Shannah said "yes Bella it is a flower (correcting Bella's mispronunciation), but what

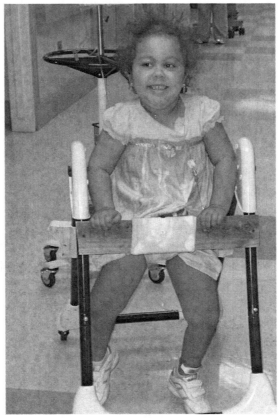

Bella Rodriguez-Torres in her walker at Miami Children's Hospital.
September 2007

kind of flower? " Bella just looked at her and responded "flowler." She did not know that it was called a rose.

That evening in the hospital after her Chemo while Bella was getting ready to go to sleep, Shannah handed Bella a rose scented Holy Rosary, Bella smelled the Holy Rosary and said in a clear voice and different tone, "Smells like roses, smells like Mommy Church." Now it has been well documented by many people who have attended places where there have been apparitions by the Blessed Mother, that the scent of roses will often fill the air. It is curious that while we did not smell the rose scent in the air, it was clear that Bella had. Even without knowing what type of flower a rose is.

Bella continued her regimen of chemotherapy extremely well with virtually no side effects. Her walking with the pediatric walker was improving dramatically. She had two more PET scans during this period; both completely clean with no evidence of cancer anywhere not even in the spine. We would continue to have a prayer teleconference before she would go into the hospital for PET scans. We continued to have a great number of people come together in prayer and reflection during these teleconferences. The army of people praying for Bella was fervent. At week 14 of her treatment, Bella's team of physicians was addressing again the subject of radiation, which according to the protocol was scheduled to begin on week 20. My father in his conversations with leaders in the field learned of a new type of radiation called proton radiation. This type of radiation is very new and at the time there were only 5 centers in the world, with 4 being in the United States. We learned that this type of radiation has much less side effects compared to conventional radiation. At that time the plan was to give Bella radiation only to the primary tumor which was presumed to be the spine as it was the largest.

Many would find it hard to believe how such cutting edge and expensive technology is guarded by many institutions to maintain high statistical rates of success. In fact we learned that unfortunately, patients that have the most advanced disease, like Bella are turned away because to put it as one center told us "when they are that far gone, we don't offer proton therapy." It was absolutely disgusting for us to believe that the patients who need the treatment most are turned away because it could negatively affect the statistics of an institution. It seems that many financial grants could be forfeited by these prestigious and renowned institutions if their success rate should fall. Of course, I suppose any institution can find good clinical results if the patients are cherry picked and not too advanced in their diagnosis. How sad, indeed, that so much of the world, even in matters of life or death, continues to revolve around money, prestige, bureaucracy and such. After much investigation and guidance by the Lord, Bella was accepted by Dr. Sameer Keole at The University of Florida Proton Institute in Jacksonville, Florida. In fact Dr. Keole's words, in contrast to others' words, were "bring Bella here; we will take care of her." After Bella's initial evaluation and simulation, we were ready to move to Jacksonville for 6 weeks so Bella could have daily anesthesia and radiation. Indeed the Lord led us to the best place; the people at the center are wonderful. They are people fulfilling their purpose of truly helping patients and putting statistics and outcomes second.

We left for Jacksonville from Miami in the evening and stopped in Orlando to pick up Kim, who would be staying with us the first few weeks to help us. Bella absolutely adores Kim and calls her "Drina" which is short for "Madrina" or godmother in Spanish. After we had dinner at Ralph and Kim's house and before we left to continue our trip to Jacksonville, Kim held Bella's hands as she stood and actually got her to take some very painstaking steps for the first time without the walker across the kitchen. You can imagine our joy, but even more, was Bella's joy realizing that she was walking, albeit with assistance. Those small steps seemed like giant leaps across that kitchen floor. Ralph, Kim, and Christian were sharing our joy and encouraging Bella to keep trying! It was an awesome moment that will never be forgotten.

We had made arrangements to stay at a Marriott Residence Inn on the south side of Jacksonville. Thanks to many generous people from work, Ralph's work, and others we were able to have enough Marriott points to pay for our long stay. The hotel was nothing fancy and it was somewhat aged, but it would be home for the next 6 weeks. We were determined to make the very best of it.

We were quite tired from our drive to Jacksonville that evening and went to sleep. We spent the next day unpacking and getting accustomed to our new surroundings. In the afternoon Shannah and I attended 5:30 PM vigil Mass at Holy Family Catholic Church on Baymeadows road. Bella stayed in the hotel room with Kim and Nelda Castillo, a friend from Panama, who came to help us during our time in Jacksonville. When Shannah and I returned to the hotel, approaching our room we could hear music playing. When we opened the door, we could not believe our eyes. Bella was dancing around the room without her walker! Kim and Nelda were so happy they were crying tears of joy. I asked Nelda how this happened. We have a black and white stencil frame of Christ that my nephew Christian gave to Bella when she was first diagnosed. We have taken that frame everywhere we've gone with Bella and have always placed it in her hospital room anytime she has had to be inpatient. We had placed this frame in the hotel room when we arrived. It was right in the middle in the living room of the hotel room on the mantle of the fireplace. When I asked Nelda, who does not speak any English, how this happened, she said that Bella had been sitting on the sofa, she pointed at the picture of Christ, said something in English, got up and started dancing around the room. When I asked Kim who speaks English, what Bella said, Kim replied "Bella pointed at the picture of Jesus and said 'Thank you, Jesus watch me!'" and began to dance around the room. Bella was now walking perfectly and she was so happy. (There is also a video of these first steps on Bella's website www.PrayforBella.com)

Bella began proton radiation therapy the very next Monday for six and a half weeks. The appointments were typically very early in the morning, which was a good thing because she could have nothing to eat prior to her radiation. The Florida Proton Center was on the north end of town, so it was important to leave early and avoid any traffic snarls. Bella was able to adjust fairly easily to getting up very early and getting in the car. Some mornings were very cold, but "Drina" would manage to throw a blanket over her head and make sure she was kept warm. Everyday she had anesthesia and radiation and afterward on some days chemotherapy. She never vomited or got sick once, she continued to be an inspiration to everyone who came in contact with her. All of the people who treated Bella in Jacksonville were wonderful. They treated her and all of their patients with absolute love and care. We also made some wonderful friends who we will have forever. Additionally, we experienced some more incredible God incidents, which I will explain in later chapters. We continued her treatment protocol of 54 weeks and later returned to Jacksonville for another 10 weeks in the summer of 2008 where the decision was made with the help of Dr. Keole to radiate all former metastatic sites. Bella handled all therapies without any significant side effects at all.

As I mentioned previously, while we were in Jacksonville, we were blessed to have made friends we will have for life. The Lord never promised us an easy road; however He did promise us angels along to way to assist us. To Goldie, Jose, Juani, Michelle, Jim, Mariola, Tony, Mary, Victor, and the many angels that came to our aid during this time; thank you! May God bless you for your generosity and love during our time of need while in Jacksonville. These people just opened their homes and hearts to us in the most caring and amazing ways. They truly exemplified love, compassion, and generosity to us, expecting nothing in return. I am sure God placed them on our road to lighten the load on our journey.

Indeed the Lord in His infinite wisdom and mercy has allowed us to enjoy Bella here in His kingdom on earth. No one can explain why Bella is alive or how she is walking, running and jumping. Bella's case defies all statistics for given the advanced stage at the time of diagnosis. The story of Bella's miracle was officially investigated by the Secretary General of the Missionary Sisters of the Immaculate Heart of Mary in Ginora, Spain. The reason for this is because one of my father's cousins is a nun, Sister Catalina Vigo in Miami. When Bella was diagnosed he immediately called her to begin praying for Bella. She and the sisters of her order began praying and have not ceased asking for the intercession of the blessed Fradera sisters, Carmen, Rosa and Magdalena, who were nuns martyred because of their faith during the Spanish War. In an order for someone beatified to be considered for canonization to sainthood, in the Catholic

Bella Rodriguez-Torres walking on her own in Jacksonville, Fl., Dec. 2007

Church, there must be miracles associated with him or her. When these amazing events began to unfold at our home, Sister Catalina asked me to document them so that they could submit this as a miracle on behalf of the blessed Fradera sisters. Thus, the Missionary Sisters of the Immaculate Heart of Mary began their investigation, and after 8 weeks, and reviewing over a hundred pages of medical records, physician's clinical opinions and other documentation, determined that they believed Bella's miracle healing was granted by God through the intercession of the blessed mother, Our Lady of Guadalupe.

Today, Bella continues to be completely back to baseline since before becoming paralyzed. Bella is in complete remission and attends school and various therapies everyday. She can run, jump, swim and dance.

Shannah completed her conversion to Christianity, was baptized in the Catholic Church on Easter vigil in April of 2008, at St. John Neumann Catholic Church. We have been so fortunate to have our family at St. John Neumann in Miami; where so many have been the face of Christ to us in our greatest time of need.

It is important for me to clarify for those who may not be familiar with the Catholic faith, that Catholics do not worship Mary. We honor her as the woman that God chose to be the mother of Jesus on earth. We believe that this was no random decision and that she played a very special role in the salvation of the world. We ask for her intercession (one who prays to God for another's intentions.), the same way anyone would ask a neighbor or a friend to pray for him or her. Bella's miracle was granted by Christ alone. Catholicism uses many visual aids which are the reason for the many statues and artwork of Mary, Christ and the saints. It is however important to know that while these visual aids help to remind Catholics to remain in a reverent and prayerful state, we do not believe in worshiping statues or any object as we define that practice as idolatry. The same way a picture of a family member or friend might remind someone of that person, Catholics use these visual aids understanding fully that like the picture of the family member or friend that the person or the spirit of that person is not in that object.

While we will never know why God chose us for this, we do know that our purpose in life going forward is to serve others in need and share this miracle with them so that they can be filled with faith and realize the many blessings, and talents we all have and to recognize the many wonderful people God puts in our lives to help us. Bella's story has touched thousands around the world. Many have come to faith or renewed faith in Jesus Christ despite any difference in way of life or denomination. Indeed "As it is, there are many parts, but one body of Christ." (1 Corinthians 10:20) This miracle happened because; thousands of people got together in prayer and stood in agreement that "NOTHING IS IMPOSSIBLE FOR GOD!" The beauty of this story is that this is a miracle that did not happen thousands of years ago. This miracle happened in modern day and to "normal people." If there has been yet another modern day example that Jesus Christ is alive, it is in the story of Bella's miracle.

My intent is that the next time you or someone you know faces a difficult situation they can reflect on this miracle and learn to say and believe: "Why not me!"

We ask that you please join the "Army of people" in prayer for Bella. We ask that you please pray for Bella and visit her website, www.PrayforBella.com to see her story, pictures and video.

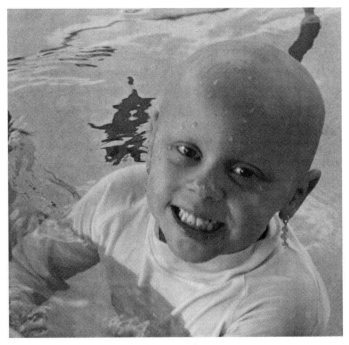

Bella Rodriguez-Torres, July 2008

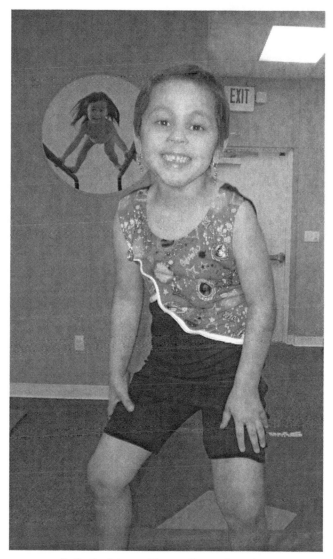

Bella Rodriguez-Torres, December 2008

THE GREATEST LESSON

As I mentioned in a previous chapter, at any point in my life if you would have asked me if I had a relationship with Christ, my immediate answer would have been "Yes!" I always had prayer in my life as taught to me by my parents and through my attendance at St. John Neumann Catholic School as a child and Christopher Columbus Catholic High School as an adolescent. I later earned my masters degree from Oral Roberts University, albeit in business management, I studied theology and learned much more about Christ. Despite this, when Bella became diagnosed, I was destroyed. It was as though I had nothing. Even though I was of supposed faith, I was alone, I was scared and I had given up.

In fact, the day we had the official diagnosis and consent to treat Bella with chemo, I was already defeated. I had already accepted that Bella was going to die. I truly believe that Satan preyed on me even further because during that time at night, after I spent several hours crying myself to sleep I would have horrible nightmares about her death. I would envision her funeral. I envisioned someone bringing me a catalog of caskets to start picking one out for Bella. It was awful. I was pitiful, mad at God and asking, "why me?" There we sat before the chief of oncology at the hospital who told us "your daughter is paralyzed and not expected to ever walk again, she has stage 4 cancer and the out look is not good." He chose his words carefully and did not say what we already knew; Bella had a few months to live. We asked him if it was even worth putting her through such torture, he said "it is worth a try." Here I am of supposed faith and yet my first response was defeat, self pity and hope that God did exist and that he heard my prayers. I suppose that in many ways my reaction and thoughts may have been typical for someone who has been given the type of news that was delivered to us.

When I reflect back on what happened to me when I spoke to my friend Tim, I learned that I was not of supposed faith, I did not doubt, but I was more than anything, hopeful. I was hopeful that God heard me, I was hopeful that everything I learned about God my entire life was true. I was hopeful that Christ was the savior of the world and that he would save my daughter. What changed was that I stopped hoping and I started believing. I learned that my hoping and "keeping my finger's crossed" was leaving room for disappointment and depression. I learned that what I had to do was exchange my hope for FAITH! I've come to believe that Hope leaves room for disappointment and fear, it is like a maybe. "I hope God is real, I hope he hears me." In contrast, Faith is absolute. It is certain and it is blind! They may seem similar, but there are huge distinctions between hope and faith!

Consider the example of the ancient Hebrews that were persecuted and slaves to the Egyptians. These were people of incredible faith. They did not hope for God to save them, they knew He would. Think about the kind of faith you need to follow an old man with a beard and a stick across a miraculously parted sea to the Promised Land! I can assure you that if that happened today things would be very different. If a crazy looking old man with a beard was on South Beach with a stick saying he was going to part the ocean, people would think he was drunk or offer to buy him another drink. Yet that did happen and those Hebrews demonstrated exemplary faith, the kind of faith we need to trust and fully rely on God.

I'm sure many reading this book have heard the term "doubting Thomas" or "Don't be a doubting Thomas" before. This term comes from St. Thomas the apostle in the Bible. On the day of Jesus' resurrection, Thomas had heard the testimony of many who had seen him and said that Jesus had come back from the dead, yet he was not sure. He had to see Jesus resurrected for himself. He had to put his fingers in his wounds to believe and be sure. Jesus did appear to Thomas and did allow him to put his fingers in his wounds. (John 20: 24-27) While Thomas has gotten the reputation as a doubter, I believe, like me, he was hopeful. Thomas was one of Jesus' twelve apostles. He saw and experienced Jesus do things that were impossible. He saw him walk on water, which is impossible. He saw him give sight to the blind, which is impossible, he saw Jesus resurrect the dead, which is also impossible, yet when people were saying that Jesus had come back from the dead Thomas was unsure. Why? Thomas had been a witness to the many miracles that Jesus had performed. Why could he not believe that Jesus had managed another miracle? In my opinion, I believe that Thomas was hopeful that Jesus was the messiah. He was hopeful that what Jesus had said was true. He probably pondered the years he spent following Jesus around Israel and thought: I hope it is true, I hope he is the one. And yet, while Jesus did allow Thomas the opportunity to place his hands in his wounds so that he would believe, what then can be said of those who did not see him resurrected, did not put their fingers in His wounds and yet they KNEW he had returned. They KNEW it to be true just like you and I know that the sun will rise tomorrow- that's FAITH. "Then Jesus told him, "Because you have seen me, you have believed; blessed are those who have not seen and yet have believed." (John 20: 29 NAB)

I've learned that Faith is not believing that God can, it's knowing that He will! Faith is not hoping that God hears us; it is knowing that He does. Further it is accepting His will and surrendering to His will that brings us ultimate peace and strength. I learned that when we ask God for something we get one of three answers: Yes, and our request is granted right away, not now, or I have something better for you.

I believe that the second and the third answers are the hardest to accept. We don't want to wait and further, we believe we know what is best for ourselves and our family. Yet if we do have faith, then we know that the Lord knows what is best for us, even if it is not what we want, He knows what is best for us. After all, He created us. After my conversation with Tim, when he spoke that word of knowledge to me, I understood that Bella belonged to God, not me. We think of our children as being ours, as being a possession. Perhaps this erroneous idea comes from the fact that our children are our DNA and we witnessed the miracle of their conception and birth. However, our children are a blessing from God. He has entrusted them to us for us to raise them, teach them, and love them. I came to realize and surrender to the fact that if God called her to heaven, there was no place better for her to be. There is no pain in heaven, no suffering in heaven and no cancer in heaven. In fact, Jesus was very clear on what heaven is - its paradise. "Then he said, Jesus, remember me when you come into your kingdom. Jesus answered him, I tell you the truth, today you will be with me in paradise." (Luke 23:42-43 NAB) When I realized this, I understood fully that Bella belonged to Him, but my only request was to please allow me to take care of her in His kingdom on Earth. Our dear merciful father granted me my request and my life's purpose now is to forever show my gratitude.

I have seen examples of God responding "Not now" both in real life and in the Bible. We have met many children who have unfortunately experienced relapse with their cancer. Unfortunately when there is a relapse, the cancer usually comes back with a vengeance. Needless to say the statistical chances of surviving of a relapse are very slim. There have been many children and their families, who we met and love, who experienced relapses and despite the statistics, are today in remission and they and their families are living testimonies to God's power and mercy. It was interesting that when speaking with these families and hearing their stories of when their children reached remission the first time, they were happy, were of faith but they had been convinced by doctors that the cancer was going to come back. The statistics said it was supposed to return and, in both cases it did, by the first scan post treatment. Yet in getting to know these people, seeing them everyday and going through treatment along with them with Bella, we noticed in these cases that something was different the second time around. They had truly surrendered by Faith to God's will. They also were thanking God ahead of time rather than seeing if God would do his thing and they would do theirs. They sounded just like the crazy guy I was when I was going around telling people that I was not going to bury my daughter! While I cannot speculate if they were more hopeful than faithful, like I used to be, I do know that God had a divine purpose and His answer to their initial prayers was, "Not now." However by faith, both of these families were given what they asked for. Both of their children are completely cancer free, despite the relapse and all explanation and statistics to the contrary.

Another example of "Not now", in my opinion comes from the bible. This passage is one that is familiar and is an obvious lesson of showing gratitude to the Lord. Yet I found another important lesson of faith. In Luke 17:11-19, we learn how there were 10 lepers who approached Jesus from a distance and asked to be healed. I found this to be a great illustration of how the Lord sometimes says "not now" to our requests. This is where we can't just HOPE he hears us; we have to KNOW he does and trust His plan for us. In this passage, while there was an immediate request for healing, it did not happen right away. These 10 had to demonstrate FAITH to the point of ridicule before it happened. During this time, people with leprosy and other illness had to live away from society in general. Only after they showed themselves to authorities and received an okay from the authorities could they rejoin society and leave the outcast society they were forced to live in. In addition, during those times, people who were deemed crazy or demented faced further persecution. For these 10 to follow Jesus' instructions and begin walking towards the authorities - at the time, full of leprosy, simply trusting his words, I believe demonstrated FAITH. Yet they asked Jesus to heal them right there and yet, he said GO - and it was when they were ON THIER WAY that they were healed, not when they asked. Although they faced potential hard criticism and further ridicule, had they gone to the authorities and been full of leprosy, they had FAITH in Jesus and blindly went on their journey. While the other 9 could have demonstrated more immediate gratitude to Jesus, Jesus' final words to the Samaritan who returned to give Him thanks, are so comforting; "Rise and Go, your FAITH has made you well."

I recently heard a story about a testimony of faith, which I think exemplifies God's response of "I have something better for you."

There was an American pilot who was shot down behind enemy lines. The pilot survived the crash but was injured and could barely walk. He saw some caves near where he was so he made his way slowly and hid in one. He could hear the enemies trying to locate him to see if he had survived, but he was too injured to run. He was a man of faith and began to pray. He said "Lord, please protect me, please build a barrier to cover this cave so that I will not be found. Shortly after his prayer, a large spider appeared and began spinning a web in the entrance of the cave. Not fearing death and fully trusting in God, he again spoke to God and said, "Lord I asked you for protection, I was thinking more in terms of a brick wall and all that has happened is this spider." That spider continued to make its web and over eight hours passed until the enemies were now inspecting the crash site and the caves. As they checked every cave, when they came across the cave with the large spider web in front of it, they shown a light and said, "don't bother checking in there, that web is perfectly intact if he had gone in that cave there wouldn't be that perfect web, besides look at the size of that spider."

The pilot was spared and while he was asking God to build him a brick wall to block the entrance of the cave, the Lord sent him something else, something better. What do you think the enemies would have done if they would have found a brick wall in front of the cave? They would have most likely blown it up, yet in His wisdom and mercy, God sent another solution a better solution, even though it was not what the pilot had wanted specifically.

I also learned that having blind faith and talking about it can make others feel that you are crazy; there is nothing wrong with that! Once I learned to transform my hope into faith, I would tell everyone and anyone that I was not going to bury my daughter! Many looked at me like I had three heads, but said kind words. While their words were kind, their body language said, "This poor man is crazy! Doesn't he know that his daughter is full of cancer?

Doesn't he realize that the statistics say that she will die very soon? Poor guy." I learned that this was perfectly all right. I learned that I had nothing to lose. I had a choice, I could go crazy because my daughter was paralyzed and full of cancer or I could get crazy about the fact that the Lord was going to save her. We live in a world of possibility. We live in a world where we are told that certain things cannot be done. Yet Christ did things that were impossible, he walked on water, which is impossible, he gave sight to the blind, which is impossible, he raised the dead, that is also impossible, yet if we believe in Him, we are called to believe in the impossible being possible. God gives possibility to the impossible, it is our choice to believe and follow that or not. One of the thoughts that I have on a daily basis, which some might consider morbid, yet it brings me great joy is that I know that Bella will be a pole barer at my funeral. She will be an old woman and I would have fulfilled my promise to God of taking care of her on His kingdom here on Earth.

Now you may be reading this and think "it's easy for you to say this given how well Bella has done. It's easy for you to say this given that you experienced amazing events with the Virgin Mary and have been blessed beyond measure by Christ." In fact you may think given what he and his family experienced, how could you not be faith filled. I agree with you! However, before any of the extraordinary events that occurred with Bella and the intercession of Mary or "Mommy Church" happened, I had to surrender, totally and completely in Faith to Christ. It is only after this that everything else started to take place.

So often in my life prior to understanding this, without knowing I would negotiate with God. Oh the mistakes I would commit and ask God to come to my rescue. My prayers were something like this: "Lord, if you please get me out of this problem, I will go to church next Sunday, if I can make it." "Lord if you please bless me with this, I will be kinder to others." Here I was asking God to show Himself to me first and then I was going to do something for him. Who was I to negotiate with God? In learning to trust Him completely I learned also to thank Him first. He knows every hair on my head; he created me and knows what is best for me despite my desires. How could He not know what I was asking him for? I learned that rather than asking him to reveal himself to me first, I am thanking Him for what he is already doing for me even beyond my understanding. I now begin my prayers in thanksgiving for everything. I don't just begin my prayers thanking Him for all of my blessings, I thank Him first for all He is doing specifically to help me in whatever particular situation I may be facing. I pray the Holy Rosary everyday and I pray in thanksgiving for all He is doing to help all of my friends and family in advance of whatever trial they might face.

Understanding the lesson of faith versus hope is as important today as it was the day I surrendered totally to the Lord and received that word of knowledge from my friend Tim. The rates of relapse for Rhabdomyosarcoma are approximately 90%. So while the statistics are again against Bella, no one can explain how Bella can walk and no one can explain why Bella is alive. We continue to claim victory in Christ for Bella.

The blessed mother, Mary was truly an example of faith. If you think of how Mary was presented with the important role she would play in salvation, it is mind bending, what a faithful Jewish mother! Here is this young woman who is unwed and is visited by an angel. The angel of the Lord tells her that she is to become pregnant by the Holy Spirit and give birth to a son she would name Jesus. The angel tells her that he will be the savior of the world. Later she would learn that he would suffer and die a horrible death. Put yourself in that position, what an incredible and difficult proposition. She would mysteriously become pregnant, how could she explain this to her family and friends including Joseph. Surely they wouldn't believe her. What an outlandish story. Yet Mary's answer was without hesitation; Yes! "I am a servant of the Lord; may it be done onto me as you have said." (Luke 1:28 NAB) As if that wasn't enough, I think about the faith of Joseph and how he must have struggled to marry a woman who was pregnant by God and not him. I'm sure the thought of another man entering the picture must have been a factor. Yet both of them were filled with faith and complete trust in God.

At Christmas time we are flooded with beautiful greeting cards and breathtaking porcelain statutes depicting the manger scene when Jesus was born. They depict cute looking animals and a very serene and beautiful scene. Yet try to imagine the real conditions in which Jesus was born. Joseph and Mary were not even able to find a dwelling fit for humans on that first Christmas Eve. Here was the savior of the world, the king of kings to be born in a makeshift barn with the nasty stench of animals, damp and cold with the elements of the night. Rather than being born in a palace with gold and expensive garments, he was brought into the world in the humblest of places. What must Mary and Joseph have been thinking? This is how we bring God's son into the world? Mary, are you sure this is true? Where are the angels and riches of heaven? And yet this is how God wanted it to be. This is how the king of kings was to enter the world and later become the greatest lesson of servant leadership the world has and will ever know.

Mary saw her son be ridiculed, beaten and be put to death in the same fashion that the worst criminals were. For what? What did He do? She stood at the foot of the cross as He died, as his mother, seeing everything unfold that she already knew would happen unfold. Yet she was chosen for this. She did not say, why me? She said, why not me!

Indeed faith is the greatest lesson I learned during Bella's illness. No matter what the Lord decides, no matter what we must suffer, I trust Him completely. While hope is good and it is necessary to have faith, hope alone leaves an open door for doubt, pain, and suffering. Faith is the only answer.

The following verse, I believe, best defines the difference between hope and faith.

"Now faith is being sure of what we hope for and <u>certain</u> *of what we do not see." (Hebrews 11:1 NAB)*

What are you hoping for? Have you been holding back to truly trust the Lord in Faith? Are you fearful to take that step because you are living in fear and hope? You <u>hope</u> that what you <u>fear</u> does not happen! Do you find yourself saying, like I used to "Hopefully things will turn out best for me." Have you ever said "I'm crossing my fingers?" I've learned that the only thing you can be sure of by "crossing your fingers" is cramped fingers. I learned that you would be better served by folding your hands in prayers of faith than just "crossing your fingers." I realize this illustration might be somewhat simplistic, however, I believe the saying "I'm crossing my fingers" is a saying that illustrates hope. Not to mention that it is nothing more than superstition that has been passed along through the ages. It is good to be hopeful and positive, but that is only half way there. Turning hope into faith and trusting the Lord fully is far more effective and gratifying. When we have faith we truly learn that God does want us to live abundantly and give us the tools and skills to have victory in everything we do, albeit those victories and abundance might be different than what we might have in mind ourselves. By faith we, like Mary, can be faced with the most difficult decisions, difficult situations and instead of saying "why me" we can say with faith, Why not me!

"Only What You Can Handle"

As I've mentioned earlier, before Bella's diagnosis of cancer, we suffered greatly because of Bella's developmental delays. Every time we would go to a birthday party or have any interaction with typical children, we would get a reminder that Bella wasn't typical in the world's perception. Additionally, when your child doesn't look outwardly mentally handicapped people can be very mean. It was very difficult. We were always frustrated with her. Shannah and I frequently bickered and prior to the birth of Rayna were on the brink of divorce. So many times I would console Shannah with her crying in my arms as she said "why, why can't we just have a normal child, why us?"

Many times in my life prior to Bella's diagnosis of cancer and the journey that ensued, I heard the term "God will only give you what you can handle." Often times when people I knew, including myself, were going through trials in life, I would hear this phrase. I hoped it was true and half heartedly bought into it. In fact, whenever I was faced with minor adversities that I felt God had helped me through, it was confirmation, I thought, for me, that God had given me that challenge because I could handle it and because he would guide me through it. When Bella was younger and before she was diagnosed with cancer, as I've stated before Shannah and I struggled greatly because of Bella's mental handicap. Yet I learned to accept

111

that God had only given us what we were prepared and capable to handle. Who better than us to tackle such a problem? In fact this is when I first thought of the phrase "Why not me!" Shannah was a former special education teacher, I had good insurance through my employer and my father and oldest brother are pediatricians, I came to accept we were better suited to deal with that problem, than most people, so why not me?

Yet when Bella became paralyzed, I looked up and asked God, "wait a minute, I can handle this?" Then stage 4 cancer, and facing the possible death of my child. "I can handle this?" It's not fair. But over the course of time and the year of Bella's treatment, we learned that we again were better prepared to handle this situation than many others. Because of my father we had access to the best medical care in the world. I had a job with a company that valued me. We were surrounded by people who loved and supported us. But, most importantly, I learned that by faith anything is possible.

I learned once you accept that God is all you have, you come to realize that God is all you needed in the first place. He gave us this challenge because we could handle it. We would find the faith to face our most difficult challenge and the resources and people in our lives to assist us.

He also gave us tremendous signs and affirmation of His love and presence. As if we did not see and experience enough, here are three examples where God affirmed that he and the Virgin Mary were with us.

When Bella was diagnosed, I sent an e-mail message to all of my customers informing them of what Bella's diagnosis was, that she was paralyzed and that I would be unavailable for the unforeseeable future. I received a very empathetic and thoughtful return message from one of my customers who told me that Rhabdomyosarcoma sounded familiar. In fact one of his closest childhood friends' daughter had died a few years back from it. He suggested that his friend and I speak and gave me his contact information. When I received this message, I was terrified. I did not want to speak to this man. For starters, I did not want to speak to a man who had lost his daughter to the same cancer Bella had. I did not want to put him nor me in a place to experience greater pain. Additionally, I did not want to boast how well Bella was doing especially since I knew his daughter had died. I did everything to avoid speaking to this man and I did for several months. My customer however did not relent. He would e-mail me periodically to find out how Bella was doing and would end each kind message with "Have you talked to my friend yet?" Every time I read those lines I would cringe. I knew that one day I would have to interact with my customer and would have to explain myself for not reaching out to his friend.

Finally one day, many months later I made the call. This is when I met Joaquin and the amazing story of his daughter Marilu. She was 18 when she was diagnosed with Alveolar Rhabdomyosarcoma; she fought valiantly for many months before the Lord called her to His kingdom in heaven. In an effort to not focus the conversation solely on his suffering I intended to ask his advice on the upcoming radiation that Bella would be having for the first time beginning on week 20 of her protocol and would appreciate any advice he could give me in his experience with Marilu.

While I had never spoken to this man before, as soon as the conversation began, speaking about Marilu and Bella, we immediately bonded. In fact, we both got quite emotional. He told me of Marilu's fight. He told me of her incredible courage and faith. He told me that her dream was to visit Hawaii and that unfortunately she passed before they could go on their scheduled trip and how he vowed to never visit Hawaii until he is reunited with her in heaven and they can look down on Hawaii together. He told me how she, despite having a tumor in her brain, undergoing chemo and radiation, was an honors student for the two semesters she was alive in college. Indeed Marilu is an angel who served as a tremendous example and inspiration to her family and many others.

I asked him a number of questions regarding the radiation. He began to explain how Marilu's main tumor was in her brain and that it would elude their efforts. Sometimes it would shrink, then it would grow or change places, it was a moving target and spread. He explained to me how Marilu was forced to wear a helmet and how the radiation was targeted to certain parts of her brain. He mentioned how terrible it was for Marilu and how she would always encourage her dad, no matter how much pain she was in, to not give up! Then he said something very interesting to me. He said "You know, while the tumor never fully went away while she was on chemo, I wish they had never given her radiation at all and just kept her on the chemo." I found this interesting because all the children I've met, other than Bella, who are on chemo suffer tremendous nausea and vomiting. I asked him, "How did Marilu tolerate the side effects from chemo?" He took a deep breath and said "Well, at first it was terrible and she would vomit everyday, but then;" (he took another deep breath and a long pause), "look I don't know of what religious beliefs you are, but you asked me the question, so I will answer truthfully." He said, "At first Marilu vomited everyday, it was awful, but then on one 12th of December, we became very devoted to Our Lady of Guadalupe. Are you familiar with the Virgin Mary?" I listened in silence and practically fell out of my chair, I simply answered "yes." He said, "We dedicated ourselves to Our Lady of Guadalupe one 12th of December, and Marilu never vomited or felt sick again."

I could not believe what this man was saying to me. I had never spoken or seen this man in my life and here he was telling me something amazing, truthfully and without knowing anything of Bella's miracle and the intercession of Our Lady of Guadalupe. I let him finish. He told me how he had, since Marilu's death, gone to the Basilica of Guadalupe and how he had no doubt that both Marilu and Our Lady of Guadalupe were watching and protecting him here on earth. He continued to give me amazing examples of how Our Lady of Guadalupe had interceded for him to find peace in his life. Once he finished, I said "Boy do I have a story for you." I told him about Bella's story about "Mommy Church" and Our Lady of Guadalupe and how Bella was born on the 12th of December.

Another example of when God gave us another sign and at the same time gave me an example of how merciful he has been with us was the following. Indeed this was a day that I understood that the Lord had given us what we could handle and not more.

There is a well-known family in our church who has a child with severe Down's syndrome. Their son is 13 years old, rarely speaks and must wear diapers. You can imagine the amazingly full daily schedule of therapies and doctors appointments a child like this demands. In addition, their youngest child had been diagnosed with Leukemia. After two years of chemotherapy for Leukemia, their son relapsed. The day I met them for the first time, they were just finishing their fourth year of treatment. If anyone had a legitimate gripe with God it would be this family.

Yet what was amazing in speaking with both the mother and father was that their cup was so filled with faith and peace, that depression, anger, sadness or resentment simply did not fit. These people in the midst of a very challenging life, had happiness. The kind of happiness that many search for, these people had. In the midst of cancer, Down's syndrome and challenging finances, these people had and continue to experience victorious joy. As I stood with the father in the hallway, talking about the hospital and other cancer related topics, there stood a man, who I did not know and had never seen prior, dressed in suit and tie with his ten year old son standing next to him. As we conversed, the man in the suit suddenly broke the conversation and pulled a ladies tennis bracelet out of his suit pocket. He put it in his hand, held it up and said "hey look, guys I have this nice women's tennis bracelet, I don't know if you guys might be interested in buying something like this?" I could not believe what I was hearing. I did not know who this man was or what he was doing here. I immediately imagined him to be a visitor of another patient. Because cancer parents are in the hospital all the time with their kids and I had never seen him, I imagined he had to be a visitor because no parent would dare do something so inappropriate as to be selling jewelry in the hospital's cancer center. Yet in an effort to be polite, I simply said, "that's nice, no thanks." This man hung his head in despair, he took a deep breath and said, "I'm sorry guys, and it's just that my financial situation is so bad that I've resorted to selling jewelry." He again put his hand in his suit pocket and said, "I don't know if you guys would be interested in this, I have some Our Lady of Guadalupe medals." I couldn't believe it. Here I am getting over the shock that this poor man right in front of his son, had to shamefully admit how bad his financial situation was, and now he was asking if I would be interested in any medals with the image of Guadalupe on them. I said to him, "Please, I would like to buy all of them." After he told me the price, I went to the ATM machine in the lobby of the hospital and pulled out a little extra cash. When I gave him the money, he refused to take the extra money. He finally agreed to take it but only if he could give me a pair of earrings for my wife.

The man left with his son and I stood in the hallway with my friend from church. He looked at me and said, "Do you know that man's story?" I said, "No, I've never seen him before." He said, "That man has six children, one of them is here with leukemia. His wife died a few months ago of a sudden brain aneurism. The reason he is in such financial problems is because all their insurance was through his wife's company, now they don't have insurance. The reason why you haven't seen him is because he has five other kids at home he has to raise and take care of. His son here is practically being raised by the nurses; it's a terrible situation." I could not believe what I was hearing. Here I was facing a bad situation, but this poor man was fighting a war for his son against cancer, grieving the loss of his wife and facing a financial crisis. This was one of the days that I looked up and said, "God thank you for my problem, I know I could not handle that."

God also put another very special family in our path, the Brennan family of Horseheads, NY. While we were building the army of people in prayer, many e-mails circulated the internet asking for prayers for Bella. Additionally, thousands of people were visiting Bella's website. The Brennan family who has a relative who works for the same company as I, began praying for Bella and expanding the army of people in prayer in their area of upstate and western New York. John Brennan and his beautiful family would post encouraging, faith filled messages almost daily on Bella's site. They also logged on to every prayer teleconference we held. One day, I finally spoke to John. I told him how I appreciated all of their prayers and support. I told him that he deserved to know the story behind the story. He and his wife Theresa were in the car on their way to visit their son Andy, who was attending college. After I told them the story of "Mommy Church", they both cried tears of joy. John, who I had never met in person explained to me that he has always had a special devotion to Our Lady of Guadalupe and believed by faith what I had told him. After our very nice conversation, we stayed in contact mostly by e-mail.

About a month later, I received an e-mail from John that their nineteen-year-old daughter, Megan, had a spring break from school coming up. He explained that as their family was sitting at the kitchen table one morning they asked Megan what she wanted to do over her spring break vacation. She answered "I want to go to Miami to meet Bella and her family." Do you think they can use any help dad?" Megan is a very kind, patient and talented young woman with a lot of babysitting experience. I answered John's e-mail letting him know that it would be a pleasure to have Megan visit and that I was sure that the girls would love a visitor. I truly did not know what to expect however, and the thought of having to play host was not ideal as Bella's daily schedule was very hectic. Nonetheless, the Brennan's entrusted their teenage daughter to travel to Miami alone and visit us. What an amazing blessing Megan has been. She loves Bella and Rayna as all of us love her. She has since come to Florida several times with and without her parents to visit and has become part of our extended family. We thank God everyday for putting the Brennan's in our life and love them dearly. This is yet another example of how people we never knew, solely because of the power of Christ came to our aid in our greatest time of need.

Before going to Jacksonville, for six and a half weeks for Bella's first round of proton radiation treatment to her spine, Shannah wanted to find a church where we could attend while in Jacksonville. She simply searched "Catholic Church, Jacksonville, FL" on the Internet. She found St. Joseph's Catholic Church. On the church's website, she found a list of ministries that had monthly meetings regarding a variety of different topics. She noticed that there was a "St. Ann's ministry" which was a group of women who all had children under the age of five. The purpose of the meetings was to share in prayer and fellowship. Below each ministry was listed the name and contact information of the ministry head. When Shannah wrote down the information to call the ministry head of the St. Ann's Ministry, she transposed the number and accidentally wrote down the name and contact information of another ministry. This is when we were first introduced to Michelle Horning. Shannah called Michelle and explained to her that she was looking to join a women's group and that we were going to be in Jacksonville for six and a half weeks for our daughter's treatment for cancer. Michelle was very kind and said she would pray for Bella and said she would love to have Shannah join her at the meeting. When we arrived in Jacksonville, Shannah called Michelle and arranged for me to drop her at her house and Michelle would drive her to the church for the meeting. We had the pleasure of meeting Jim, Michelle's husband, Isabella, her daughter and Michael, her son. In the car on the way to the church, Michelle asked Shannah how she found her. Shannah explained that she had seen her name on the church's website as the ministry head of the St. Ann's ministry. Michelle said "Oh, I am not the ministry head for that, I am the head of a different ministry. It just so happens that because Michael is under five, I also attend the St. Ann's meetings." When they arrived at the church, Michelle showed Shannah a beautiful mosaic of Our Lady of Guadalupe and explained that their church was very devoted to her. Shannah was in disbelief. She told Michelle the amazing story of Bella and "Mommy Church." Michelle explained further that their parish had such a devotion to Guadalupe that they had a pilgrim image of the *tilma* that the parishioners rotated among the families throughout the year. A family would take the image home for a week and pray the Holy Rosary together every night during the week. Michelle later explained incredibly that she and her family were scheduled to have the image on the 12th of December, on Bella's birthday and the feast of Our Lady of Guadalupe.

We became very dear friends of the Horning's and they lent us the image to have in our hotel room while we were in Jacksonville on the 12th of December. Here was a woman and a family we had never met telling us of her and their churches devotion to Our Lady of Guadalupe. Coincidence perhaps; we think not. The Horning's had a Birthday party for Bella while we were in Jacksonville. They had many faithful friends come as we all prayed the Holy Rosary together and celebrated Bella turning five and the feast day of Our Lady of Guadalupe. Yet another day we claimed victory in Christ!

One of the lessons that I believe exemplified the term of "God will only give you what you can handle", for me was never having to answer certain questions. Shannah and I did suffer a lot with Bella's mental handicap and severe language delay. As I've stated earlier, the social component of dealing with this was very hard and frustrating. While it continues to be less of a problem, it became such a clear blessing of how God shielded me from something I know I could not handle.

While Bella's severe speech and comprehension delays were such a problem earlier in her life, they became such an enormous blessing later. Bella has never asked me the question "Daddy, am I going to die?" She never asked me "Daddy why do you take me to these places to have the doctors do all these horrible procedures to me?" And yet over the course of meeting other parents, I have personally met fathers that have had that question posed to them and have had to answer. I thank God that I have never had to answer those questions. All the time that Bella was under treatment, she did so with a smile. Yes, she cried and was scared but she never stopped being joyful and a wonderful example of strength to all who came in contact with her. Even when she was paralyzed, she would simply smile in her wheelchair and tell the other children and adults, "I slipped." I feel as though God shielded me through Bella's mental handicap of much emotional injury I would have had to face otherwise. Indeed, God only gave me what I could handle.

When Bella was declined proton radiation therapy at one center, the Lord lead us to Dr. Sameer Keole and the University of Florida Proton Institute. As I mentioned prior, the people there took excellent care of Bella. Our relationship with Dr. Keole began as a typical doctor patient relationship, however it quickly evolved into a friendship. He invested himself personally in Bella and remains so happy at how, against all odds, Bella is doing so well. This culminated with him coming to our home on a social visit to simply hang out. He brought his son Shaan to play with Bella and Rayna in our swimming pool and barbecue in the back yard. During his visit he explained to me many things that I was unaware of.

When he accepted Bella as a patient at the proton center, he had not checked with the team or his supervisors first. When he presented Bella's case to the team at a tumor board, they were concerned about accepting her. She was a high-risk patient and the likelihood of her survival was grim. He understood their concerns but he said that there was something about Bella's case that kept him up at night. He said additionally that there was a problem that had occurred with the anesthesia team who sedates the children at the proton center, which put a cap on the number of children that they would accept as patients. In fact he said that the problem was such that they had considered no longer treating pediatric patients at that time. Dr. Keole personally took it upon himself to approach the anesthesia team and explain that there was one specific patient he had to get in. He negotiated a plan with the proton center and anesthesia to include Bella. He convinced the proton team that while traditionally protons where not used in the most severe cases like Bella's, that he believed that she was precisely the kind of patient who needed this new and innovative treatment. With his persistence and his faith that Bella would get better, he got Bella in. He says that he does not know why he fought so much for Bella in particular, he hadn't for any other patient prior, but he felt there was something different about her. Moreover he said that Bella's incredible positive outcome was helping him and others change the paradigm of only using protons on patients with high chances of survival. Indeed many other children with cancer who would have not been offered this important treatment now will be. Dr. Keole continues his passion for treating children, especially those who are considered most difficult to treat. He is a man of great compassion, and we thank God everyday for putting him in our lives.

Today I not only hear "God will only give you what you can handle", and believe, but I tell others that I believe it to be true. I have had the displeasure of meeting many parents who have lost their children to pediatric cancers and while their grief and pain is inexplicable, these people tend to be the people at greatest peace; often times it is those around them who are falling apart. I am convinced that for anything you may face in life, there is a divine purpose for. We seldom realize what the purpose is, yet everything has a purpose and I believe nothing to be simply coincidence, I believe in "God-incidence."

When we may be faced with a problem, no matter how big or small, when we truly take stock of who we are, what we are blessed with, those we have around us, we can believe that by faith there is nothing that cannot be overcome. In fact as I initially looked up and said, "God I can not handle this!" and later found out how we were better equipped than most to handle our greatest challenge. You can find the same in any situation you may be facing life. There is nothing impossible for God and if we can surrender to His purpose by faith, we will prevail. In fact, God gave us free will. It is in the moments that are most difficult in life that we have a great choice to make. Will I let this overwhelm me? Will I allow depression and negativity to surround me? Will I spend my time talking to others and partaking in the 'misery loves company crowd.' I can assure you that you will first agree with me and second, not find anyone who has ever truly benefited from making that choice. It is easy to fall into that trap. Many of the problems we face in life are exceptionally hard and unfortunately many people relish seeing others depressed and down. However, it takes the same amount of energy to get depressed and defeated about something as it does getting determined and focused on overcoming the problem. So often, we will also decide to put our own ending on how the situation will end. It's important that we don't put a period where God is only placing a comma. We need to put our trust entirely in God and do our part as well. It's our choice. How will you choose the next time you or someone you know is faced with a tough situation?

The next time you are faced with a tough situation rather than asking God, "why me?" Say "why not me!" Know that God hears you rather than hoping that He does and walk in victory by faith!

"Therefore I say to you, all things for which you pray and ask, believe that you have received them, and they will be granted you." (Mark 11:24 NAB)

"God's gift to you is who you are, your gift to Him is who you become."

APPENDIX
ACTUAL MANUSCRIPT OF BELLA'S MIRACLE

The following is a timeline of events regarding inexplicable events, healing and visitations of the Blessed Mother to Bella Rodriguez-Torres. Bella is a 4 ½ year old girl, born on December 12ᵗʰ 2002. Bella was born with Periventricular Leukomalacia (strokes in the white matter of the brain); which has caused her to be developmentally delayed. She has also been diagnosed with a severe speech delay. She is the daughter of Raymond (32 years old; Roman Catholic) and Shannah (31 years old; Jewish converted to Catholicism on (3/23/08). They and their younger daughter Rayna (2 years old) all live together in Miami, Florida.

On July 20ᵗʰ 2007, Bella was diagnosed with stage 4 Alveolar Rhabdomyosarcoma with PAX 3 translocation, which according to experts and Bella's doctors, put her in the worst prognostic setting for survival. The primary tumor was around the spinal cord which caused her to be paralyzed. The neurosurgeon informed the parents that he did not believe Bella would ever walk again. "Anything she does not do currently, she will probably not do after surgery." She also was found to have 7 other metastasis throughout her body; in her jaw, shoulder, hip, rib, knee, hand and foot.

Immediately following diagnosis, Raymond's father (Ramon Rodriguez-Torres, MD) called Sister Catalina Vigo of the Sisters of the Immaculate Heart of Mary in Miami, Florida asking them to please pray for a miracle for Bella. The nuns of this order immediately began praying for a miracle through the intercession of Sisters of the Immaculate Heart of Mary, specifically the martyred Maria del Carmen, Rosa and Magdalena Fradera Ferragutcasas, Spanish, religious of the Congregation of Daughters of the Blessed and Immaculate Heart of Mary, killed during religious persecution in Spain in 1936, who were beatified by Pope Benedict XVI on 10/28/2007. The prayers for the intercession of the beatified have not ceased.

Date   Occurrence

Sunday- 12ᵗʰ of August 2007   *Bella was discharged from Miami Children's Hospital at approximately 7:00 PM. At time of discharge, the parents were informed that she was scheduled for outpatient chemotherapy on Tuesday the 14th; however her Hg was 7 and her WBC was 1,700. The physicians who discharged Bella informed the parents that more than likely she would require a transfusion as it was nearly impossible for her levels to be elevated enough to allow her to take chemotherapy on Tuesday.*

The Sisters of the Immaculate Heart of Mary continuously ask for the intercession of the Fradera sisters for the miracle cure of Bella.

At approximately 11:30 PM EST, at home, asleep and in the dark, Bella awoke and in a tone and vocabulary not typical of her, told Shannah "Mommy, the Church carries me" "The Church takes care of me." Upon hearing this, Shannah asked Bella who had told her that and Bella replied "Her." At this point, Shannah turned on the lamp near the bed and asked Bella again, "Who told you that?" Bella pointed without hesitation to a picture of the Virgin Mary on the dresser in the bedroom. Shannah picked up the picture, brought it closer and then asked Bella, "She told you that?" Bella answered, "Yes."

A few minutes later Bella, who was completely paralyzed, moved her leg and foot, hit Shannah, and proclaimed, "I did it!" She then turned again to Shannah and spoke in vocabulary not typical of her, "The booboos are not all gone yet, but will be very soon."

Bella went to sleep and Shannah began to quietly pray the Holy Rosary. Bella awoke, grabbed the Holy Rosary from her hand and said "Mommy that's hers."

Monday- 13th of August 2007	*In the morning Bella said "Mommy Church will help me walk again soon."*
	During the morning the parents asked Bella about Mommy Church. The parents decided to show Bella different pictures of the Virgin Mary. She said that she was wearing red and had a baby. The parents eventually showed her a picture of our Lady of Guadalupe and she identified her as "Mommy Church" and the baby as the angel under Our Lady's feet.
	At approximately 11:00 PM while asleep, Bella screamed out, "No!!, I want to sleep with Mary!"
Tuesday- 14th of August 2007	*At Bella's doctor appointment, everyone was surprised to find that in less than 48 hours, Bella's Hg level had risen to 10 and her WBC level had risen to 12,900. This meant she did not need a transfusion and could continue with her chemotherapy.*
	During the afternoon while at Miami Children's Hospital, Bella told her 19 year old cousin Christian, "Mommy Church will help me walk again soon." She also said, "I saw the angel walk through the wall." Christian asked where this happened and Bella answered "At the hospital." Christian asked if the angel had wings; Bella answered "No."

126

During the night, Bella screamed out *"Thank you Jesus, help me walk again!"*

In the parking garage of Miami Children's Hospital at approximately 10:30 AM EST, Bella told her father Raymond, in words and a tone not usual to her, "Mommy Church is going to help me walk very soon."

Shannah and Raymond attended Mass at St. John Neumann Catholic Church on the Feast of the Assumption of Mary at 7:00 PM. During the homily given by Monsignor Pablo A. Navarro, (pastor of St. John Neumann Church) Shannah says she had a vision of the Blessed Mother carrying Bella and presenting her to Christ. Shannah claims that Jesus looked at her and said, "I will save her but you must serve me."

As soon as the Mass ended, Shannah told Raymond that she wanted to convert to Catholicism and expressed what she had experienced.

After the Mass, Raymond and Shannah approached Monsignor Navarro and they briefly explained what had been happening at their home with Bella. Monsignor Navarro visited their home around 9:00 PM and prayed with them and over Bella.

Thursday- 16th of August 2007	*In the night, Bella screamed out, "I love you Jesus, thank you!"*
Friday- 17th of August 2007	While playing *with her cousin, Christian, Bella was suddenly able to sit up for the first time.*
	At approximately 12:30 PM, Bella told Christian, "Mommy Church takes care of me; she is my mommy; she helps me"
	Before going to bed, Bella told her parents, "When they take the pictures; Booboos all gone."
Saturday-18th of August 2007	*Bella continues to refer to pictures of Our Lady of Guadalupe as "Mommy Church."*
Monday- 20th of August 2007	*Bella's parents and godparents hosted a prayer teleconference with Fr. Gregory Parkes from Corpus Christi Catholic Church in Orlando, Florida. There were over 100 participants praying in unison.*
	At the chapel of the Sisters of The Immaculate Heart of Mary, the Sisters of the order prayed the Holy Rosary and the Office of the Liturgy of the Hours before the blessed sacrament and made special petitions to the martyred sisters Fradera for a miraculous cure for Bella.

Tuesday- 21st of August 2007	*Bella has an MRI, which reveals that the primary tumor around the spinal cord has been reduced 94% having had only 5 weeks of chemotherapy of the 54-week protocol. Her doctors had said prior to the test that should the MRI show that the tumor had not grown it should have been considered a step in the right direction. The tremendous reduction is completely atypical of a Rhabdomyosarcoma stage 4. Prior to the MRI, her oncologist had suggested not doing the test, as it was not expected to see any changes from baseline so early.*
Thursday- 23rd of August 2007	*Bella has a PET Scan to see the effect of the chemotherapy on the rest of the metastasis specifically her jaw, shoulder, rib, hip, knee, hand and foot. As Bella was sedated and undergoing the exam, her oncologist stated that while he was extremely pleased with the results of the MRI on Tuesday, we should not expect any changes in the metastasis because those in bones like these respond even more slowly to chemotherapy.*
	As Bella was going through the PET Scan, Raymond and Shannah prayed the Holy Rosary in the lobby of Miami Children's Hospital. During the prayer, Raymond felt a voice tell him, "They will look and not find it." Raymond promised, if it was so, to visit The Basilica of Guadalupe in Mexico City the following week to give thanks.

The conclusion of the PET Scan was that no visible metastasis could be detected. The only tumor that was visible was the tumor around the spinal cord, which had been significantly reduced.

Sunday-26th of August 2007

In the evening, while laying with Raymond under the covers in bed, Bella again spoke in atypical tone and vocabulary and said,
"Very soon Daddy," When Raymond asked "very soon what?" She said "Mommy Church, help me walk very soon."

Twenty five minutes later, while asleep, Bella suddenly awoke and screamed, "I love you Jesus!"

Wednesday- 29th of August 2007

As Raymond approached The Basilica of Guadalupe in Mexico City and got his first glimpse of the buildings, Shannah called him to inform him that at that very instant Bella who had no mobility of her legs, began to crawl all around the home, at approximately 10:35 AM EST.

Sunday- 9ᵗʰ of September 2007   *Because of Bella's mental handicap, she suffers from a self-regulation disorder. During one of the manifestations of this, including pulling out her hair in the master bedroom with Raymond and Shannah present, Bella suddenly stopped crying and having a fit. She sniffed the air and said "I smell roses." Raymond and Shannah were instantly surprised as Bella has never been able to identify different types of flowers and has never said the word rose. She did this at approximately 9:30 AM and later at approximately 7:30 PM, in the same location in the bed of the master bedroom.*

Tuesday- 11ᵗʰ of September 2007   While hospitalized for chemotherapy, a nurse at Miami Children's Hospital entered Bella's room with a rose in her pocket. Shannah asked if she could borrow the rose and showed it to Bella. She asked, "Bella what is this?" To which Bella eventually replied, "a flower." Shannah again asked what kind of flower?" Bella did not answer.

That evening, around 9:00 PM, Shannah held a Holy Rosary and passed it to Bella. Bella sniffed the Holy Rosary and said, "smells like roses, smells like Mommy Church."

131

Saturday- 3rd of November 2007	*The Sisters of the Immaculate Heart of Mary continue their prayers and supplications for the complete and total cure of Bella to the now beatified Sisters Fradera.*

As Shannah and Raymond attended Mass at a local church in Jacksonville, Florida, Bella stayed at the Jacksonville Bay Meadows Residence Inn, as she was to begin six weeks of radiation treatment on her spinal cord. When Raymond and Shannah returned, Bella, for the first time was able to walk without assistance and was dancing around the hotel room. According to Kim Rodriguez-Torres and Nelda Castillo, who were present, Bella was sitting on a sofa, pointed to a picture of Jesus in the room and proclaimed, "thank you Jesus; watch me!" She then began to walk and dance alone.

Wednesday-19ᵗʰ of December 2007

After recovering from her regimen of daily anesthesia and proton radiation at the University of Florida Proton Institute in Jacksonville, Florida, Bella tells Shannah, "I see Grandma in the light," "Grandma has a port like me." (referring to her medi-port)

Shannah's paternal grandmother, Beverly, died of cancer in 1997. Bella never knew Beverly and there had not been any recent discussion about her and never had there been a conversation that she had a port as described by Bella.

Monday- 28th of January 2008 *Bella, again in a tone and vocabulary not typical of her, tells Shannah, while hospitalized for chemotherapy at Miami Children's Hospital, that "Jesus made all the "boo boo's" go away." She told Shannah that Jesus had kissed her on her forehead and that "Mommy Church" was with him." She later said she saw angels. Shannah asked Bella about a girl, (Mariett) who had died in the hospital, unbeknownst to Bella. She asked her if Mariett is with Jesus to which Bella answered, "yes."*

As of the date of this documentation, Bella is in complete remission from cancer, and can run, jump and has complete command of all her limbs. Shannah completed the RCIA program (Rite of Christian Initiation for Adults) and her conversion to Catholicism at the Easter Vigil Mass on 3/23/08. Prayers to the beatified Missionary Sisters of the Immaculate Heart of Mary Maria del Carmen, Rosa and Magdalena Fradera Ferragutcasas, killed during religious persecution in Spain in 1936, continue for their intercession on behalf of Bella.

We certify that the aforementioned events and dates are accurate as of 10/24/08.

Raymond Rodriguez-Torres, M.mgt   **Shannah Rodriguez-Torres**

CPSIA information can be obtained at www.ICGtesting.com
Printed in the USA
LVOW061703301111

257214LV00004B/135/P